Course Design

NEW DIRECTIONS IN LANGUAGE TEACHING
Editors: Howard B. Altman and Peter Strevens

This important series is for language teachers and others who:
– need to be informed about the key issues facing the language teaching profession today;
– want to understand the theoretical issues underlying current debates;
– wish to relate theory to classroom practice.

In this series:

Communicative Language Teaching – An introduction
by William Littlewood

Developing Reading Skills – A practical guide to reading comprehension exercises *by Françoise Grellet*

Simulations in Language Teaching *by Ken Jones*

Video in Language Teaching *by Jack Lonergan*

Computers, Language Learning and Language Teaching
by Khurshid Ahmad, Greville Corbett, Margaret Rogers and Roland Sussex

Beyond Methodology – Second language teaching and the community
by Mary Ashworth

Course Design – Developing programs and materials for language learning *by Fraida Dubin and Elite Olshtain*

English for Specific Purposes – A learning-centred approach
by Tom Hutchinson and Alan Waters

Principles of Course Design for Language Teaching *by Janice Yalden*

Strategic Interaction – Learning languages through scenarios
by Robert J. Di Pietro

Self-instruction in Language Learning *by Leslie Dickinson*

Understanding Research in Second Language Learning – A teacher's guide to statistics and research design *by James Dean Brown*

Focus on the Language Classroom – An introduction to classroom research for language teachers *by Richard Allwright and Kathleen M. Bailey*

Course Design

Developing programs and
materials for
language learning

*Fraida Dubin and
Elite Olshtain*

CAMBRIDGE
UNIVERSITY PRESS

Published by the Press Syndicate of the University of Cambridge
The Pitt Building, Trumpington Street, Cambridge CB2 1RP
40 West 20th Street, New York, NY 10011-4211, USA
10 Stamford Road, Oakleigh, Victoria 3166, Australia

First published 1986
Sixth printing 1992

Printed in the United States of America

British Library cataloguing in publication data

Dubin, Fraida
Course design: developing programs and materials
for language learning. – (New directions in
language teaching)
1. English language – Study and teaching –
Foreign students   2. Curriculum planning
I. Title   II. Olshtain, Elite   III. Series
428.2'4'071   PE1066

Library of Congress cataloging in publication data

Dubin, Fraida.
Course design.
Bibliography: p.
Includes index.
1. Language and languages – Study and teaching.
2. English language – Study and teaching – Foreign
speakers.   3. Curriculum planning.   I. Olshtain, Elite.
II. Title.
P53.295.D8 1986   428'.007'1   85-25525

ISBN 0-521-25676-3 hardback
ISBN 0-521-27642-X paperback

Contents

Contents

≫→

Contents

Thanks

Many of the ideas in *Course Design* have come about through our individual experiences gained from teaching in master's degree and workshop programs for people in both ESL and EFL settings. We acknowledge the inspiration, stimulation, and feedback which our students at the University of Southern California, the University of British Columbia, Tel-Aviv University, and Harvard University gave us when these chapters were in their developmental stages.

In addition, we acknowledge with gratitude the insightful comments and suggestions on the first draft of the manuscript of 1983 given us by Marianne Celce-Murcia, Lola Katz, Shirley Ostler and Kari Smith, which led us to this final version in January 1985. Ahsile Nibud extended expert graphics counsel in the preparation of the diagrams.

Introduction

1 Instructional planning and English language teaching

At various times during their careers, professionals in the field of language teaching find themselves involved in tasks quite removed from actual classroom instruction. Among these non-teaching assignments are the planning of courses and the writing of materials. Both require specialized background of a kind which is commonly glossed over lightly or benignly ignored in too many university programs in applied linguistics, English language teaching and teacher training. Yet, graduates of such programs are often called upon to fulfill course design tasks without having received the proper training to do so. Throughout these chapters, we have tried to maintain the point of view of designers and writers rather than the one more frequently employed, that of teachers, the objective of this book being to enable teachers to expand their expertise so as to become course designers. We have done this deliberately – and we hope consistently – because we feel that it is a view which has been undervalued and relatively unexplored.

Since the planning of courses and the writing of materials is a sparsely documented area, designers and writers have tended to work on the basis of their best intuitions. Fortunately, people who design language courses are usually thoroughly familiar with what goes on in classrooms. However, designing courses which will be used by other teachers or writing textbooks for a wide and unknown audience is different from planning one's own teaching. Therefore, it is necessary to use a different frame of reference, to acquire new perspectives from which to see the issues.

The very complexity of human language together with the wide variety of circumstances in which it is taught may partly explain why the field of language pedagogy has paid comparatively slight attention to the basics of course designing and materials writing. Instead, it has stressed the activities of single teachers and their students, as evidenced by the long history of methodology directed at this audience alone. Among other reasons, this concentration on the individual pedagogue has tended to keep second and foreign language specialists from paying much attention to the well-developed field of general curriculum construction outside ESL. For its part, the general curriculum field, in the United States

1

at least, has only been concerned with foreign language teaching (typically of major European languages to American students); English as a second language is such a newcomer in North America that some in the educational system believe the letters 'ESL' stand for one, particular methodology.

2 General curriculum planning

As background information for second and foreign language course designers, a brief review of a few of the outstanding contributors to the general curriculum planning literature is warranted. Taba's outline (1962:12) of the steps which a course designer must work through to develop subject matter courses has become the foundation for many other writers' suggestions. Her list of 'curriculum processes' includes the following:
1. Diagnosis of needs
2. Formulation of objectives
3. Selection of content
4. Organization of content
5. Selection of learning experiences
6. Organization of learning experiences
7. Determination of what to evaluate, and the means to evaluate

Adapted to English language teaching matters, her list, although suggestive, is not sufficiently explicit regarding the area of language content. Nor does it allow for a distinction between broad, national goals for courses in multilingual contexts and narrower course objectives for the teaching of actual language skills and competencies.

Another writer who also has written on general curriculum designs, McNeil (1977:1), offers guidelines for planning which are extremely valuable for identifying the role that a curriculum plays in establishing the intellectual backdrop or policy for instructional plans. He categorizes recent curriculum designs in the United States under four general headings based on their educational-cultural orientations: humanistic, social-reconstructionist, technological, and academic subject matter. Any one of these orientations could serve as the basis for a curriculum for a language program. However, since McNeil's model is not specifically concerned with language programs, what is lacking is some mechanism for including a theoretical view toward language and language learning.

3 The aim of the book

The chief purpose of this book is to present an overview of the course designer's task, beginning with its most fundamental aspect, societal needs assessment, then working through curriculum and syllabus construction, finally coming to the stage of materials preparation. In relation to materials, a few selected aspects of the craft of writing are illustrated. In following this outline, we have drawn on the steps proposed by Taba, applying her suggestions in the context of second and foreign language teaching. To formulate this comprehensive view of designing for language learning, we have established certain basic definitions of key terms: 'curriculum', 'syllabus', 'goals', 'objectives', and 'needs'.

The terms 'curriculum' and 'program' are used interchangeably in this book to describe the broadest contexts in which planning for language instruction takes place, either on the national level or for a community's schools. A 'syllabus', on the other hand, is a more circumscribed document, usually one which has been prepared for a particular group of learners. In some places, the terms syllabus and course outline mean the same thing, although recently the term syllabus has taken on a special meaning concerning the specification of language content alone.

Although the terms 'goals', 'objectives' and 'needs' are apt to be used without regard for the important distinctions among them, a model for designing language programs should set them apart. Goals address more general, societal, community, or institutional concerns. In developing a language curriculum, issues concerning language planning and policy must be taken into account since it is the society or broader community which the program serves that fundamentally determines the goals to be manifested in the course. In an ideal situation, thus, goals are determined by carefully examining information about the patterns of language use within the various domains of the society, as well as by studying group and individual attitudes toward English and toward all other languages which are used in the setting. We have also used the term 'societal needs assessment' in relation to determining program goals.

A curriculum which is not in line with the broader community's concepts of language education, certainly one which does not accommodate the immediate audience's expectations – those of teachers and learners – may just gather dust on a shelf. Such could be the fate of a document which reflected the latest discussions of professionals in language teaching/learning circles yet which did not include sufficient explanations for local teachers who were asked to use it. In many ways, curriculum designers must constantly juggle and balance the disparate aspirations, opinions, and beliefs of all of those groups that look to the document they produce for guidance and inspiration.

Objectives, in turn, are specific outcomes or products of courses which are outlined in a syllabus. Objectives guide teachers; they also help learners understand where the course is going and why. Objectives can be expressed in terms of proficiency scores, or as performance objectives such as language skill attainments: a reading rate of so many words per minute with X% comprehension, or the ability to write a five-paragraph composition with acceptable sentence and paragraph sense. Setting objectives in the course plans makes it possible to carry out the necessary evaluation measures. It also makes it possible to specify the various levels of instruction within a program. Course designers ideally make use of information from all interested sources when they write objectives: learners in previous courses, teachers who are ESOL specialists, teachers in other subject areas – all those in the institutional setting who share an interest in the program.

Needs, on the other hand, are associated with individual learners. Since they change and shift during the period of a course, needs are best addressed at the level of classroom instruction, where a teacher can select appropriate techniques and materials to accommodate individuals. From the course designers' point of view, however, the crucial factors are those that must be determined before the learners arrive. Since a curriculum and a syllabus are documents which are produced to guide teachers and learners, they must be in place and ready to be used before learners and teachers meet together on the first day of the program.

4   Practical applications

An important part of each chapter in *Course Design* is called '*Practical Applications*'. These sections have been included to involve readers more personally in the topics presented, giving them an opportunity to consider the issues through their own experience and background. Although the Practical Applications sections are intended to augment university courses and workshop sessions, individual readers will find that themes developed in each chapter are carried into the Practical Applications section in more concrete form.

References

McNeil, J. D. 1977. *Curriculum: a comprehensive introduction.* Boston: Little, Brown and Company.
Taba, H. 1962. *Curriculum development: theory and practice.* New York: Harcourt, Brace and World.

1 The fact-finding stage: assessing societal factors

Overview

Before initiating a new language program, vital preparatory work in the form of information gathering must take place. This fact-finding stage provides answers to the key questions in any program: Who are the learners? Who are the teachers? Why is the program necessary? Where will the program be implemented? How will it be implemented? The answers to these questions, in turn, become the basis for establishing policy or formulating goals.

The first two of these key questions deal with the audience for whom the program and materials are to be developed, the actual consumers of the new program – teachers and learners. To know who the teachers and learners are requires thorough attention to needs assessment of a societal nature. Just as in the business world, market research has become an essential ingredient for commercial success, so in curriculum design, the fact-finding stage is an imperative prerequisite for effective decision-making regarding the participants.

In a country or setting where the language program planners and designers do not know the existing conditions, the fact-finding process must rely heavily on basic sociolinguistic research which relates to national concerns, international ties and political trends. However, in those places where the planners are conversant with local conditions, they may be able to supply the answers to some of the questions them-selves, or at least be able to call on other specialists who can provide the necessary information.

Assembling data bearing on these factors is usually carried out by means of two basic techniques: collecting information that appears in governmental and other institutional documents, for example in census reports, and administering questionnaires and interviews which collect both objective and subjective feelings and attitudes prevailing among the members of a community. However, in those places where the planners are conversant with local conditions, they may be able to supply the answers to some of the questions themselves, or at least be able to call on other specialists who can provide the necessary information.

In order to answer the key questions inherent in the fact-finding stage, investigations are necessary in each of the four areas specified in diagram

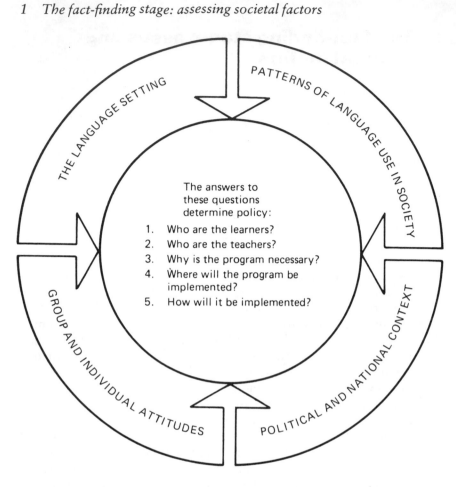

Diagram 1   The fact-finding stage
The fact-finding stage provides answers to key questions about language
program policy.

1. Accordingly, this chapter comprises four major sections: 1.1 The
language setting; 1.2 Patterns of language use in society; 1.3 Group
and individual attitudes toward language; and 1.4 The political and
national context.

1.1   The language setting

The term language setting refers to the 'totality of communication roles'
(Gumperz 1968) in any speech community. Program planners need to

understand and evaluate the significance of the language setting in terms of its effect on the learners and the learning process. For example, the language setting might be one in which there is strong support for the learning of the target language (TL). On the other hand, it could be one in which there is indifference or even negativism towards it. Therefore, an initial survey of the language setting should provide a description of the role of the target language and the roles that all other languages fulfill in the local community.

There are a number of basic ways of characterizing language settings. One important distinction derives from the role of the TL. Where English is the TL, there are differences depending on whether English is also the language of a wider community (often called English as a second language or ESL) as opposed to other types of settings where another language or languages are spoken by most members (English as a foreign language or EFL). Additionally, the roles in which language functions in the English speaking community need to be carefully investigated. For example, in a bilingual situation in an English-dominated country, the language or languages of ethnic groups may predominate in interpersonal functions in home and family life. On the other hand, in a non-English speaking setting, it is important to establish the role of English in respect to all other languages in the country.

While in an English speaking setting the language goals are often associated with the overall acculturation process (Schumann 1978) of new immigrants, migrant workers, or with specialized courses for foreigners who spend a limited amount of time in the country, the goals for learning English in a non-English setting are often closely related to the community's overall process of modernization. The phenomenon of 'shrinking world' has intensified the already existing need for a common world language – an international language – often referred to as a 'language of wider communication' (LWC). An LWC or world language is vital for communities whose primary languages are not widely used outside their own area. People of such communities need an LWC for purposes such as foreign trade or in order to gain access to scientific, technical and literary materials that do not exist in their own languages. Even when such an LWC fulfills major functions within the community itself, for example, when it has official or semiofficial status, its major role is closely linked with the process of modernization.

1.1.1 The continuum: ESL——EFL

Language settings where English is the TL might also be viewed along a continuum. At one end of the continuum is an English speaking setting where the language is spoken natively by most of the population, examples are the United States, the United Kingdom, and Australia. Moving slightly away from that end of the continuum, there are countries in which English is one of two or more official languages spoken natively by at least part of the population – Canada, South Africa, and others. Further along, there are countries where Engish is the only official language but is not the native language of more than a small minority of the people – Nigeria, Uganda, Zambia, and others. Most of these countries have maintained English (the language of the former colonial power) as their present LWC, both for international needs and for internal communication among speakers of different languages.

Moving further along and approaching the other end, there are countries where English is neither the national language nor one of the official languages, but is given special status because of historical factors such as ex-colony or mandate status, or because of social and economic reasons: Israel, Kenya, Ethiopia, Malaysia and others (Fishman et al. 1977). In some of these countries English is the medium of instruction in the school system, or at least for a part of the course of study, while in others it only has the status of a major foreign language, one which is compulsory and highly valued as a prestige subject in the curriculum. Finally, at the other end of the continuum there are countries where English is taught as only one of several foreign languages available to students within the school system, even though in practical terms it may be recognized as the most important foreign language: Japan, People's Republic of China, Italy, Brazil and others. Even in these cases, the role of English in the process of modernization, science, and technology is significant.

The position of the particular language setting along the continuum is an indication of the degree of support which the learner can find in the immediate environment. The highest level of support is, of course, available in an English speaking setting while the least is in the case where English is no more than a school subject. Yet, affective factors related to learners' attitudes might interfere with the students' exploitation of the support available in the fully native setting or may interfere with the effective implementation of a new program in a school system where the feelings of the population are anti-target culture for political or national reasons. Although the language setting itself is very significant, it cannot be fully evaluated without taking into account other factors that impinge upon it.

Adult language learners in an English speaking setting can be of two broad types: (a) those who have come to settle in the new community and whose first needs are survival skills, and (b) those who have come for a limited period of time, probably for a well-defined purpose. In the case of the first group, learners' needs and expectations must be considered in relation to their potential employment either as professionals, skilled or unskilled workers. Of course, planners who have implemented such adult ESL programs know all too well that in any one group of learners there can be a wide range of both language and educational backgrounds among the participants.

In the second instance, the relevant language setting may be limited to the school or community within which the students will live for a short period. Learners may be enrolled in a summer course or in a program offering an academic degree or certificate. In both cases, the assessment process must involve faculty and fellow students in these courses in order to help the planners recognize requirements as articulated by the school environment.

Finally, the English speaking setting might also be the environment in which students from other countries come for ESP (English for Special or Specific Purposes) courses. Thus a group of bankers, for instance, may go to England for an intensive course of three to six weeks. This course might focus on the English language needs of banking clerks when functioning in their own environment – in the non-English speaking context. Yet, while they are in England, it will be necessary to take full advantage of the setting. Consequently, needs must include the type of extra-curricular activities that these students will want to participate in outside the actual course of study although their stay within the target speech community is temporary and the need for acculturation is limited.

1.2 Patterns of language use in society

Among the basic types of language settings, we have distinguished between an English speaking setting and all the others, or those places in which English plays different roles as evident in the various types within the EFL range in the continuum. The common element among these other settings is the fact that English plays the role of an LWC, but this role can vary considerably from one setting to the next. Societal needs can only be defined for these settings on the basis of a careful investigation of the role of English as an LWC. Such an investigation must examine three major areas: (1) the role of the LWC in education, (2) the role of the LWC in the labor market, and (3) the role of the LWC in furthering the process of modernization.

1.2.1 Education

In education, for any setting where English is not the native language of most members in the community, two major aspects need to be considered: the role of English as a means for furthering one's education, and the effectiveness of the existing curriculum and teaching materials. The first and broadest question relating to the role of English in the process of furthering one's education is whether English is the medium of instruction in the school system. The question to ask is: do students study geography, math, and other general subjects in the native language or in English?

Not all cases where English is the medium of instruction are the same. In some countries the medium of instruction is the native language only in the early years of schooling, while English becomes the medium in secondary school and in others English is the medium of instruction only at the college level. In other cases, English as a medium of instruction is limited to certain subjects for which there may not exist suitable teaching materials. In Malaysia, for instance (Boey 1979), at the time when the country gained its national independence in 1957, the primary school offered six-year courses in four languages: Malay, English, Chinese and Tamil; but it was written into the constitution that Malay would become the national language and English would be the official second language. Thus the educational system began a transition period switching gradually from English to Malay as the medium of instruction, reaching a stage at which only tertiary education still maintained English as a medium by 1982. At this point, many educationists realized that the level of English proficiency, as was to be expected, decreased and therefore some suggested that English be reinstated as a medium of instruction at least for some of the subjects.

In order to evaluate the true role of English in the school system, it is necessary to have a full picture of all subjects taught at school and of all available textbooks and other teaching materials. In addition, if teachers are not native speakers it is important to evaluate their knowledge of and ability to use English.

Another question arises in cases where English is not the medium of instruction: what is the role of English as a language of study? This question refers to the degree to which the learners depend on their knowledge of English in order to get access to the subject matter of their interest. For example, what level of English competence is actually necessary for a person to study engineering at the college level? Are there any textbooks, lectures and other study matter in the native language or is it all available in English only? English as a language through which to learn advanced subjects is sometimes referred to as EAP (English for Academic Purposes) but, in fact, the scope of learning a language for studying is wider than that of an academic context since it may also include scientific and technological subjects which are not taught at the college level. For example, courses in vocational or technical schools might make use of texts and manuals written in English.

Once the role of the LWC in education is established, it is necessary to evaluate the effectiveness of the existing program and materials. Often a new program is required because there is a serious gap between the results of the existing one and the needs of learners for English as a language of study. Policy decisions will have to be made in order to find ways to close this gap, if indeed it has been determined that learning through the English language is a worthwhile educational goal in the society.

An indication that language programs are failing to meet learners' objectives is often signaled by the existence of flourishing schools and courses outside the official educational system. In these instances, graduates of the formal school system enroll in private courses because they feel that they lack the level of proficiency needed on their job. In Thailand, for instance (British Council English Teaching Profile 1979), English has been a compulsory subject but was changed to an elective subject throughout the school system. Thus, the national educational system has not placed great emphasis on English and as a result the level of English is lower than what the public feels it needs. There is, therefore, a growing demand for English classes outside the school system. Various institutions of academic or professional types offer courses in English to teachers, scientists, business executives and others.

In many countries, colleges and universities offer special preparatory and remedial English courses to all graduates of the school system because universities do not accept them as being sufficiently advanced for studying at college level. Such a situation indicates a sharp discrepancy between the achievements of the English instructional program and actual societal needs.

Information concerning the effectiveness of the existing program in the school system comes from two major sources. One is through examining the official documentation available and the other is by an investigation of the English program itself. As far as the first source is concerned, in most cases the ministry of education in a country can provide the relevant information, often even with results of surveys and research that already has been carried out. In some countries, there are special research institutes which carry out various surveys within the school system that might be of great value to the investigators dealing with the LWC situation. In other cases, universities are involved in various research projects that may throw light on the questions relating to curriculum design.

In addition to consulting the official documentation, it is usually advisable to conduct a survey of the English program itself containing evaluative mechanisms for finding out about: (a) the results of language achievement tests, (b) the overall curriculum, (c) the existing textbooks, (d) the existing teaching methods, (e) teacher-training programs, both in-service and preparatory, and (f) opinions and perceptions expressed by teachers, students and parents.

The combination of the two paths of investigation, official documen-

11

tation and careful evaluation of the existing program, provides a picture of the effectiveness of the English instructional program at any point in time. Such an investigation may take several weeks, several months or several years, depending on the scope of the study, the size of the community, the degree of cooperation of local authorities, the participation of suitable personnel, and the available funding.

1.2.2   The labor market

In collecting information about the role of the LWC in the labor market, the researcher needs access to official assessments from governmental or other labor agencies, but in addition it is vital to interview and collect information from individuals in the field. Such field reports should include employers, employees, as well as those who are job seekers. It might be relatively easy to get information from governmental offices such as a ministry of labor (where there is such an institution or its equivalent), or national employment agencies, governmental productivity and labor research institutes, and the like. But in addition to these 'state' agencies, it is important to obtain views from general employment agencies, as well as from placement centers for professionals, technicians, and academics.

From all these institutions, the researcher should inquire:
1. Which professions require a knowledge of the LWC and to what extent:
   a) the need for speaking?
   b) the need for writing?
   c) the need for reading professional material?
2. To what extent do the people seeking employment have the required knowledge of the LWC?

Newspapers and advertisement columns seeking and offering employment are another good source for checking the labor market. In addition, advertisements of institutions of adult education reflect what people are seeking, in terms of language courses, once they have completed their schooling, and after they have had experience in the labor market. These data serve to reveal the gap between the school system and actual needs that school graduates face.

Finally, interviews with individuals who have been absorbed into the labor market in a variety of professions, and with others still seeking employment, should be held. Information gained from the first group makes it possible to assess the real requirements for the LWC in the field and learn to what extent it aids or hinders one's professional progress. The second group – those seeking employment – provides a useful, up-to-date picture of:
1. how well prepared they are in the LWC.
2. to what extent they expect to use the LWC.

1.2.3   The process of modernization

The important factors affecting the role of English in the process of modernization are closely related to the accessibility of technological information and know-how. To what extent is such information accessible to a community whose primary language is not an LWC? In this context, several questions need to be considered:

1. To what extent are technological and scientific journals available in the local language(s)?
2. To what extent are instructions and catalogues accompanying modern machinery made available in the local language(s)?
3. To what extent do professionals receive training abroad?
4. To what extent is the community dependent on assistance given by foreign experts?

In a rapidly developing society, these four factors are most important in terms of developing human resources of high caliber to help implement technological progress. If, however, such materials and instruction are not available to the members of the community in their own language, a first prerequisite will be the acquisition of the LWC as a tool to further one's knowledge in technological and scientific fields. If the LWC is not readily available to large parts of the population, then neither will advanced technology be available to them, unless special efforts are made on a national scale to translate important reading matter into the local language or languages.

On the basis of information collected about patterns of use of the LWC in a particular community, a definition of societal needs can be made. Such needs will thus be defined in terms of the concrete, practical ways in which the members of the community use or need to use the LWC, for example, in relation to questions such as: In what contexts will a person need to use the language? What will be the extent of this use in terms of reading, speaking, writing? What levels of proficiency and accuracy will be required?

1.3   Group and individual attitudes toward language

Societal needs can be investigated and evaluated qualitatively and quantitatively, yet their effect on the actual success of a new program cannot be determined without taking into account group and individual attitudes towards the learning of an additional language. Whether the setting is a native speaking environment or not, it is important to distinguish between two types of attitudes: (a) attitudes towards the TL, the people who speak it and the culture which it represents; (b) attitudes towards the learning/acquisition process itself, its relevance to individually perceived needs, its efficacy as represented by the teachers, the materials and the school system as a whole. The first type usually reflects group attitudes while the second type is an indication of personal factors based on an individual's experience and aspirations.

Positive attitudes towards the language will reflect a high regard and appreciation of both the language and the culture it represents. Positive attitudes towards the acquisition process will reflect high personal motivation for learning the language, a feeling of self fulfillment and success and an overall enthusiasm about the language course. A combination of positive group attitudes towards the language with positive individual attitudes towards the process is believed to bring about the best results in terms of language acquisition.

Negative group attitudes towards a language are often related to historical factors, political and national trends, or social conflicts. In a country that was colonized, for instance, the attitude of the members of the community might be anti-LWC because it represents the earlier colonizing power. This might create a clash between such group attitudes and the real needs of the nation for an increased use of the LWC for instrumental purposes. Similarly, in an English-speaking environment, a group of new immigrants might develop negative attitudes toward speakers of English who act superior, either socially or culturally. Such an atmosphere can influence newcomers to emphasize self-identity and group congruence by placing high value on maintenance of their first language and limited, instrumental acquisition of the TL.

Negative individual attitudes may have their initial roots in negative group attitudes, but these can become intensified by negative experience with the acquisition process such as classroom anxiety, feelings of discrimination, and the like. The combination of negative group attitudes with negative personal feelings will result in the lowest level of language acquisition. Negative attitudes, whatever their roots, create psychological distance between the learner and the subject matter and are, therefore, of vital significance in the learning-teaching process. In such cases we may find ambivalent attitudes on the part of learners who realize the necessity to learn and use the LWC but have developed negative feelings towards it.

A conflict between individual or group attitudes as based on learners' perceived needs and the specified goals of the existing program might be another source of negative feelings. If the course of study emphasizes either a literary or structural analytic approach to language learning while learners feel that they need to use the language for immediate communicative purposes, there may be a serious conflict of interests which will affect the learners' motivation.

Learners' negative attitudes can be detrimental to the success of the language program. Course designers need to place special emphasis on attractive materials and involving tasks which will gradually help change learners' attitudes at least towards the learning process. However, when there is a conflict between individual and group attitudes, course designers need to look for approaches to learning which will be acceptable to both. Whenever policy makers are aware of individuals' and the community's attitudes towards the language program, they can look for suitable solutions in their new designs. Therefore, one of the outcomes of the fact-finding stage is to make planners aware of existing feelings in the community.

Since attitudes can only be inferred from behavior, attitude assessment can never be exact. Yet despite the complexity of the task, attitude assessment measures such as questionnaires and interviews are commonly used tools for collecting data. In one type of questionnaire, the investigator makes an evaluative hypothesis as to the kind of response that a certain attitude will bring about. In other words, the investigator predicts the behavior resulting from a pre-supposed attitude, then expresses it in the form of a question to which the subject responds. In this case, the wording of the question is quite crucial. Most of what we are concerned with in attitude assessment has to do with the subject's covert and only partially conscious thoughts and feelings. Yet, for lack of better and more reliable tools, we must resort to attitude questionnaires and interviews which utilize overt processes.

The questions which appear on an attitude questionnaire can be phrased directly to focus on the issue under investigation, or indirectly to indicate tendencies but without fully spelling out the point in question. Direct questions have the advantage of being easy to interpret and evaluate. Their disadvantage lies in the fact that the respondents are not always completely frank and open on the issue at stake. Respondents may choose to tell what they think the investigator would like to hear rather than what they truly believe. Thus, for instance, if we want to find out whether English is the preferred foreign language in a country where three foreign languages are taught, a direct question can be asked:

Rate the following three foreign languages in terms of importance.
1 – very important
2 = important
3 = not very important

English ....

French ....

German ....

The answers to this question will be easy to evaluate and quantify, but one is never sure that the answers are truthful. Therefore, it may be necessary to add a series of questions which seek out true feelings about the language without stating the fact so directly. If high correlation is found between the direct and indirect questions, the results can be considered more significant. But indirect questions are much harder to formulate. If we want to find out whether there is a definite preference for one of the three languages, we must look for instances where such a preference might be expressed in the subjects' environment. Do they, for instance, prefer books, films, journals, music, or other such elements in one of the three languages? We can see how we have already greatly complicated the interpretation of the answers that we might get. If people prefer films in English, is it because of the language or because of the level of cinematography? How do we interpret such answers?

Ideally, a questionnaire should contain direct as well as indirect questions on each important issue that is being investigated so that the correlation or lack of it will help the researcher evaluate the results.

If one wants to evaluate the degree to which students at the high school level view English favorably (where English is taught as a FL), direct questions relating to this issue could be:

1) How do you feel about your English class?
2) Why is it important for an educated person to know English?
3) How do your friends (peers) feel about English?
4) Have you ever studied English privately? If yes, what was the reason or purpose?
5) Would you like to be more proficient in English? How would you go about obtaining your goal?

On the other hand, indirect questions can be written so that the word 'English' does not appear, but the interpretation of the answers will indicate to some degree whether the student views the TL positively:

1) Who are your favorite pop-singers?
2) Who are your favorite authors?
3) Which is your favorite school subject?
4) Which is your favorite TV program?
5) Do all your friends speak (L1) natively? If not, what languages do they speak? (particularly important in an English language setting)
6) Which language would you like to know well in addition to your own?

As stated above, all of these questions are shown in the 'open' form: the respondent writes in a full answer. This type of question is not always best for the kind of information being sought since the results are both difficult to quantify numerically and to interpret in a significant manner. A preferred method, therefore, is to 'close' questions as often as possible. Sometimes it is advisable to begin the investigation with a small, pilot sample utilizing only open questions. On the basis of the answers to the open questions, a better closed questionnaire can be designed since some of the answers can serve as choices. In most cases, however, it is quite simple to change an open question to a closed one. The question about 'liking the English class' mentioned above can be rewritten as:

How do you feel about your English class?
.... I like it very much.
.... It is not very interesting.
.... It is boring.
.... I hate my English class.

Obviously this question is much more suitable for quantification but it tells less about each individual student. Thus, it is common to have most questions on an attitude questionnaire of the 'closed' type with just a few left open, allowing free answers to provide the investigator with information to support the interpretation of the other questions.

From this discussion, it is clear that attitude questionnaires cannot give all the answers and cannot give completely accurate ones, yet the information which they provide the researcher is vital in the stage preceding actual planning and curriculum decision making. Perhaps the most important value of questionnaires is that they help the investigator to know the target audience better.

1.4   The political and national context

Political, national, and economic considerations are closely interlaced with each other and can even be viewed as one composite element, but at the initial, fact-finding stage, it is necessary to devote attention to each of these factors separately. Viewed at the highest level, political considerations have to do with the particular regime or administration in power and how it views the question of language in general. In the native-English setting, laws and regulations concerning bilingualism and language maintenance of minority groups are significant in their effect on the type of courses given within the school system. Allocation of funds for teacher training programs, relevant research programs and material development projects will all depend on the priorities set up by the administration in power at a particular point in history.

In an LWC setting, national considerations might be particularly important for countries which are still grappling with nationhood. Forming a new political state is closely linked with establishing a national language. Therefore, during the early period, all educational resources may need to be directed to the development and promulgation of the national language. Priority may have to be given to the national language at the expense of the LWC, even if, in terms of economic efficiency, it would be more advantageous to supplement the spread of the LWC. Or, in the early stages, different languages may prevail in different domains. For example: (a) various local languages for early education; (b) the preferred national language for intermediate education; (c) the LWC – an international language – for government and higher education.

If the preferred national language is resented by some of the groups within the national entity, the process of establishing it as a full primary language will be slower. This may allow the LWC to gain considerable strength and become the language of the educated classes, as had happened initially in the Philippines and Ethiopia. On the other hand, when the new national entity is not multilingual in nature and when the area has been colonized (or under mandatory rule) by the speakers of the LWC, the tendency might be to reject the LWC in the initial years of statehood and direct all resources to strengthening the national language, as was the case in Israel and in most North African countries. It is, therefore, easy to see how at times a conflict might arise between the need to develop international ties on the one hand and create social integration, on the other.

Sometimes strong nationalistic feelings call for maintaining purity of the national language. This often brings about a lessening of emphasis on the LWC and an intensification of the local language. In many societies, a manifestation of this tendency is the strong resistance to the assimilation of borrowed terms from a world language. Modern classical languages usually try to draw terms for new concepts from their ancient variants or mother languages rather than allowing free borrowing: Romance languages from Latin and Greek, modern Arabic from classical Arabic, Hindi from Sanskrit, and so on. Such trends usually lessen the importance of the LWC, even at the expense of economic development and technological advancement, by creating a discrepancy between the needs as perceived by the public and the policy as made by governmental institutions.

When initiating new curriculum design or launching a materials development project, planners must be fully aware of the political and national priorities prevailing in the community at that particular time. In decision making, all these factors must be taken into account. The following chapters will incorporate such factors into the development of new programs.

Practical applications

IN AN ENGLISH LANGUAGE SETTING:

1. Select a well-defined audience from a homogeneous language background, a community which is trying to establish itself in an English speaking community. (For example, Vietnamese, Cuban, Pakistani.)

a) Interview some people who are enrolled in an ESL course to find out what they perceive as their language needs.
b) Find out what communicative roles are fulfilled by English and what roles are carried out in the native language.
c) Interview a few leaders in the community and compare their views of newcomers' needs with what you gathered in (a) and (b) above from students in an ESL class.
d) Discuss your findings with the other participants in the workshop and make up a list of recommendations for the policy-making stage.

2. Locate a course given to a group of people who have come for a limited length of time. Evaluate the course after working through the following steps:
a) Interview the teachers and the director to find out what the stated goals are.
b) Interview a number of students to find out what they think about the course. On the basis of their comments, work out a 'closed' questionnaire on the students' attitudes toward the course (personal attitudes) and give it to all the students who are enrolled.
c) Evaluate the materials used in the course, first in the light of what you found out in your interview with teachers and the director in (a) above, and then in the light of your interview with students (b) above.
d) Draw up a list of suggested changes which you would recommend on the basis of your findings.

3. Interview selected personnel in an employment agency to find out what language requirements are specified for non-native speakers with respect to different jobs.

4. In an academic setting: Interview key university professors to find out what level of English they expect their students from non-English speaking countries to have.

5. Make up a list of hypotheses of what you think the attitudes of the community you investigated in 1 above might be towards English. Draw up a suitable attitude questionnaire.

IN AN LWC SETTING:

Following is a suggested inventory for a description of language in education. Complete the information in this inventory according to the situation in your own community. Form teams so that participants work on different parts of the inventory. Then, discuss the findings with your colleagues.

Language in Education Inventory: The Role of English

English in the Public School System:

1. English is taught as:

    a) The medium of instruction ....

    b) FL 1 (1st foreign language) ....

    c) FL 2 ....

2. Is English a compulsory subject? ....

3. Teaching of English begins in grade ....

4. Number of weekly hours devoted to English ....

5. Official examinations ....

6. Teachers' level of proficiency ....

7. Teachers' training and certification ....

8. Textbook used in the school system ....

English in Private and Special Schools:

1. Percentage of private schools as opposed to public schools ....

2. Types of private schools ....

    ....

    ....

3. The pupil population: numbers/social stratum/etc. ....

    ....

    ....

4. The status of English in these schools ....

English as a Language of Study:

1. To what extent is English required by the institutions of higher education? ....

2. Are English courses given at the university? ....

3. Are any regular courses given in English? ....

4. How significant is English in professional courses? ....

English Outside the School System:

1. Courses for adults:

   a) Number ....

   b) Types of courses ....

   c) Student population ....

2. Courses organized by economic enterprises and ....
   other professional institutions (e.g. banks, etc.) ....

Is English Effectively Taught as a School Subject?

1. Results of the in-depth survey carried out within the school system:
   (interviews with teachers, principals, inspectors)

   ....

   ....

   ....

2. Information gathered from official documents:

   ....

   ....

   ....

3. Results of the survey on public opinion: (interviews with parents, graduates
   of the school system, the public in general)

   ....

   ....

   ....

References

Boey, Lim Kiat. 1979. 'Issues in the teaching of English as a second language in Malaysia'. In Feitelson.

British Council. *English teaching profile 1979.*

Feitelson, D. 1979. *Mother tongue or second language? On the teaching of reading in multilingual societies.* Newark, Delaware: International Reading Association.

Fishman, J. A., R. L. Cooper and W. W. Conrad. 1977. *The spread of English: the sociology of English as an additional language.* Rowley, Massachusetts: Newbury House.

Gumperz, J. J. 1968. 'Types of linguistic communities'. In Gumperz 1971.

Gumperz, J. J. 1971. *Language and social groups*, pp. 97–113. Stanford: Stanford University Press.
Schumann, J. H. 1978. 'Social and psychological factors in second language acquisition'. In J. C. Richards (Ed.) 1978. *Understanding second and foreign language learning*. Rowley, Massachusetts: Newbury House.

Other suggested readings

Gardner, R. D. and W. Lambert. 1972. *Attitudes and motivation in second language learning*. Rowley, Massachusetts: Newbury House.
Harrison, W., C. H. Prator, and R. G. Tucker. 1975. *English language policy survey of Jordan: a case study in language planning*. Arlington, Virginia: Center for Applied Linguistics.

2 The basis for curriculum and syllabus designing

Overview

The next task for course designers is to interpret the results of the fact-finding stage by making operational decisions. First, they use the information gathered in order to set broad policy: what are the significant, overall objectives of the language program? Second, they define the audience as fully as possible: is there a uniform group of learners who will use the program or are there sub-groups such as ESL (English as a second language – in the natural setting of the target language), EFL (English as a foreign language) or ESP (English for specific purposes)? Third, they consider how the program can best be suited to the particular school system, community, or language course. Local tradition may suggest to planners that the new program should focus more on either language analysis or language use. All of these three broad areas which result in concrete decisions are discussed in section 2.1 *Establishing realistic goals*.

Section 2.2 *Surveying existing programs* presents a situation in which there is an existing syllabus, textbooks, and other materials. In this case, the new program may come to replace an older one, it may just be added to the existing ones, or it may be presented as an experiment to enable policy makers to choose the best program once they have all been evaluated with each other. In any of these cases, course designers need to be familiar with the existing materials. New decisions cannot be made without fully understanding the existing situation.

Section 2.3 *When the materials in use constitute the curriculum and syllabus* suggests ways in which to examine the degree of compatibility holding between the materials in use and the explicit – when there is such a document – or implicit syllabus. In considering situations in which there is no curriculum or syllabus, course designers must rely solely on textbooks in use as sources of information which indirectly suggest program goals and objectives.

Finally, section 2.4 *The separate purposes of a curriculum and a syllabus* establishes basic definitions for a curriculum and a syllabus, the documents which course designers produce. Having established these terms, they are used accordingly throughout the ensuing chapters.

2 The basis for curriculum and syllabus designing

2.1 Establishing realistic goals

The information gathered during the fact-finding stage is utilized by a policy-making authority whose job it is to prepare guidelines for new courses. At the national level, the authority might be a curriculum advisory committee, while at the local level it could be a teachers' committee assigned the task of preparing a new program. In either case, the process requires translating societal needs and expectations into operational and attainable goals. In the case of the advisory committee a draft document specifying overall educational goals would be prepared, then passed on to a syllabus committee. In the second case, the teachers' committee would prepare both the specifications of the goals and the course syllabus with its more specific objectives.

2.1.1 In an EFL setting

A document stating national priorities usually defines goals in very broad terms, allowing for more specific decision-making to be carried out at lower levels. Such a wide, general view is illustrated in the following statement which might occur in an EFL setting: 'The purpose of introducing an additional language into our educational system (provided it is a world LWC) is to allow communication with the rest of the world.' This statement of objectives reflects overall societal goals for a country which needs to promote contacts with other communities. On the other hand, if the particular educational system places high priority on personal aspects of language learning, a statement like the following might be found: 'The main objective in learning an additional language is to allow for personal growth and enrichment.' Both of these quite general statements might lead policy makers towards different types of decisions. The first strongly emphasizes the need for communication, while the second emphasizes individual choice and achievement.

If the emphasis is on the communicative aspect of language learning, or in other words on the learners' ability to use the target language for communicative purposes, then planners are likely to design a utilitarian-oriented syllabus, one which encourages the development of communicative-type teaching materials. In more operational terms, the curriculum committee might define the terminal goal of the program as follows: 'The student finishing this program will be able to converse effectively with a native speaker on topics of interest, will be able to read authentic materials for pleasure or professional needs, and will be able to correspond with friends, colleagues or business associates in the target language.' This definition is still very general, but it is an attempt to give some description of the terminal competencies which are the expected outcome of the course.

In some countries, general goals of a language program might be defined more narrowly if the system has different types of schools, for example: academic high schools, scientific high schools, vocational high schools, etc. In such cases, it would be necessary to define the terminal competence of the graduates of a vocational high school, for example.

On the basis of the broader goals, it is necessary to set up a number of intermediate objectives in an attempt to specify expected outcomes at each stage. If English as an additional language is taught starting in junior high school, for instance, it may be necessary to specify the objectives for those finishing junior high and leaving school, as well as for those continuing with their studies. These would then be intermediate objectives for some students and terminal ones for others.

It becomes important to investigate the societal needs of such potential 'school leavers', while at the same time it is necessary to define 'entry knowledge' to the high school level for those continuing with their studies. In order to set up proper objectives for these two populations, as well as to develop suitable batteries of achievement tests, it is imperative for planners to interview both teachers and students at the junior and senior high school levels, along with graduates of the junior high school who may have taken on various jobs in the community and would be able to indicate their needs for English outside the school system.

2.1.2   In an ESL setting

Although individual needs and wants must be taken into account in both EFL and ESL settings, they are more pronounced in the ESL one in those cases where learners have moved to a new environment in which the target language plays a crucial role in the overall process of acculturation. In the ESL situation of this type, the broader goals may simply state the most idealized outcome for a language course: 'learners are expected to eventually use the language as "near" native speakers.' Yet, the learners might be painfully aware of immediate, daily needs in order to begin to function in the new community, needs which are quite removed from this ideal terminal outcome but which are vital for daily survival. In this kind of situation, courses for both children and adults must set up goals to fit individual needs and wants by reflecting social objectives as well as academic, professional or occupational ones.

Young learners in second language situations, too, have dual needs. First, to learn those school subjects which are part of the general curriculum for their age group (science, history, math, etc.), but also to be able to participate in the social life outside the classroom. The goals of a language program, therefore, must account for both academic and social-survival needs.

Adult learners in higher education also have dual needs: on the one hand they must cope with English in classes in their field of interest. For this purpose, their academic needs might be defined in terms of both language and general learning skills such as understanding lectures in the target language, taking notes, reading textbooks, etc. On the other hand, these students often have strong needs to acculturate and socialize in the new community. Again, the course must set up goals that incorporate both academic-professional and survival situations faced by students.

2.1.3   Planning for courses outside the school system

As a final example of how goals are established to fit broad needs, consider a typical ESP (English for specific purposes) course which might take place in either a foreign language or target language setting. These courses are often financed by the participants' employer. Therefore, the overall goals are set up by the employer's representative. In a course for 'management English', for instance, the stated objectives might be for learners to develop the following abilities: (a) to negotiate in English with clients, (b) to correspond with foreign companies, (c) to lead business meetings in English, (d) to develop a richer business vocabulary, (e) to communicate over the telephone, etc. However, the participants may feel that their ability to cope with such routine matters in English is quite sufficient, but that they need more general fluency so that they can also chat with their clients or business associates before and after business meetings. For such a course to be successful, it is necessary to broaden objectives to include both the company's requests and the participants' own personal agendas.

2.1.4   Language analysis or language use as course goals

Within any setting, when designers sit down to establish goals they are influenced by current trends in the language teaching profession. These trends are the intellectual background against which decisions are made. Of course, trends tend to shift over time. Actually, through the long history of language teaching in western civilization, orientations have fluctuated as educational outlooks and aims have shifted. In cyclic fashion, goals have alternated between periods when teaching languages for purposes of social use or performance was favored and times when teaching languages as vehicles for analysis or as providing access to literary and philosophical pursuits prevailed (Kelly 1969, Celce-Murcia 1980). So, for example, in both the Middle Ages and again in the seventeenth and eighteenth centuries, language pedagogy emphasized teaching about the structural properties of classical languages, particularly Latin and Greek, as model systems of argumentation and literary form.

During any particular period, designers and pedagogues quite unconsciously tend to adopt orientations which either emphasize language analysis or use since these views are tied into cultural beliefs about the educational objectives of the society as a whole. When a 'language analysis' approach is favored, emphasis is placed on grammatical analysis and on language philosophy. When 'language use' is favored, the focus is on utilization of the target language for actual communication. In our own time, although occurrences of both language use and analysis can be found, the objective of learning a new language for communicative use is generally valued over that of learning about analyses of the target language. At the same time, interest in analysis, both of particular languages and of human language in general, is the focus of professional linguists and academic departments of linguistics.

A problematic area for course planners and materials writers is that of using the output of linguistics or the analyses of language as the sole or even primary input for course designs and materials. A scientific grammar, which is the objective of theoretical linguistics, must be translated into a pedagogical grammar before it can be used for materials development. Such a pedagogical grammar takes into account the learning process, interference from the first language, complexity of forms, frequency of occurrence, and other relevant factors which bear on the acquisition of the new language. It guides course designers in what forms to select for primary focus, and what contexts to use in order to facilitate acquisition. All of these considerations need then to be put through the filter of 'learner needs'. The result may look very different from the scientific grammar which served as a starting point.

2.2 Surveying existing programs

Most new programs are designed either to remedy the deficiencies in existing ones or to expand and improve them. It is imperative, therefore, to begin any new endeavor with a thorough survey of existing conditions. In describing a program currently in operation, five basic components of the program should be examined: (a) the existing curriculum and syllabus, (b) the materials in use, (c) the teacher population, (d) the learners, and (e) the resources of the program. Such an investigation is guided all along by one fundamental question: 'In what ways has the program succeeded ... failed?' Only by understanding the strengths and weaknesses of the existing program can a better one be developed.

2.2.1 The existing syllabus

The syllabus, the first component to be examined, is the vehicle through which policy-makers convey information to teachers, textbook writers, examination committees, and learners concerning the program. No matter what its title, of course, it is the content of the document which concerns program designers, not what it might be called in a specific setting. For what we are calling 'syllabus' might have the title of 'curriculum', 'plan', 'course outline', or any number of other names. Whatever it is called, it is a document which ideally describes:

1. What the learners are expected to know at the end of the course, or the course objectives in operational terms.
2. What is to be taught or learned during the course, in the form of an inventory of items.
3. When it is to be taught, and at what rate of progress, relating the inventory of items to the different levels and stages as well as to the time constraints of the course.
4. How it is to be taught, suggesting procedures, techniques, and materials.
5. How it is to be evaluated, suggesting testing and evaluating mechanisms.

When a syllabus is available, it becomes a useful starting point in surveying the existing situation. Often, however, an initial inspection of the syllabus may reveal that the document referred to as a 'syllabus' fails to supply the necessary information. It may be too general, lacking details essential for course planning at the local level, leaving both teachers and course designers without any direction. If this is the case, one may expect to find a lack of cohesiveness in materials and examinations used within the system.

Alternately, one may find an elaborately detailed syllabus, but there may be a problem with some or all of its components. The course goals may, for example, be unrealistic, a situation often found in countries where English, formerly the official language, has been downgraded to an LWC but the terminal goals have not been adjusted. Similarly, such a situation might be typical of the goals of a one-semester course for foreigners where the planners expect full communicative ability, but in terms of available time this is a completely unrealistic goal.

Some section of the curriculum or syllabus should reflect the philosophical and educational approach that guided the policy-makers. But such an approach may be outdated or unsuitable for learners' present needs. Thus the inventory of items may not suit current thinking in language pedagogy or it may not suit societal needs as discussed in the previous chapter. If this discrepancy is discovered in examining the syllabus, the next step in the investigation is much clearer, since the effect of the syllabus on selecting and developing materials and on teacher training is of utmost significance.

Certainly, one might easily imagine a situation in which there is no existing syllabus. In many ways, such a situation is preferable from the point of view of the course designers since then syllabus specification becomes an integral part of the larger task of course design. On the basis of the information gathered in the fact-finding stage, designers would produce a document which answers all the questions specified in this section.

2.2.2 The materials in use

In surveying the existing materials, it is necessary to develop questions as an aid for evaluating them. The following questions are suggested as a minimal set:

1. By whom and where were the materials developed: by a team of materials developers who are familiar with this particular educational system and student population, or were they produced for the international market which at best is concerned with the broadest possible definition of the target population? If the latter is the case regarding all or most of the existing materials, this may be the central drawback in their design.

2. Are the materials compatible with the syllabus? Compatibility should be evidenced for all the points specified within the syllabus. Similarly, the procedures, techniques, and presentation of items must be in harmony with the specifications given in the syllabus. When such compatibility exists, the job of surveying the existing situation is relatively easy since the conclusions drawn from an examination of the syllabus would also apply to the materials. However, if the materials are not compatible, they may need to be evaluated separately.

   Examples of non-compatibility may often be found in materials which exhibit more awareness of new approaches and learners' needs than the syllabuses on which they are based. This happens when planners of policy are reluctant to incorporate new ideas and trends before they have been carefully experimented with and found suitable. Materials, under these circumstances, often fulfill the function of experimentation with new ways. The opposite can also occur: a new syllabus which is to serve as a basis for new materials will often incorporate the latest developments in the field of language teaching while the existing materials still reflect earlier versions of the syllabus. This is usually typical of an interim period before sufficient new materials are produced.

3. Do most of the materials provide alternatives for teachers and learners? Alternatives may be provided in terms of learner-tasks, learning styles, presentation techniques, expected outcomes, etc. This is a significant feature of effective materials since not all types of learning routes are suitable for all learners. When there are no built-in

alternatives which allow teachers and learners to choose what suits them in their particular situations, then the materials might be imposing and restricting rather than allowing for expansion and enrichment. Ideal materials should present teachers and learners with a jumping-off place, a stimulus for the learning process at each point. Effective materials should enable experienced teachers and autonomous learners to develop their own alternatives according to their needs and personal preferences.

4. Which language skills do the materials cover? Are they presented separately or are they well integrated? Materials often reflect the developers' preference for some language skills at the expense of others. If this is compatible with the overall goals, for instance such general goals might specify the fact that learners do not require any proficiency in the writing skill, then this would be a suitable realization of the syllabus. If, however, there is a lack of integration which is independent of the specified goals, then this might be a very serious drawback of the materials. A good example of such a situation is the discrepancy between goals which might specify the need for promoting listening comprehension and materials that ignore this point completely.

5. How authentic are the text types included in the materials? This may be a very crucial question especially in cases where texts might have been adapted for a variety of purposes. Thus, a spoken dialogue which is only read by the students in written form without an aural version might be greatly deficient. Similarly, if a textbook contains only re-written, watered-down stories that were adapted for the particular text, students using that material may never have the opportunity of encountering authentic text. Furthermore, variety of text types might be very significant in exposing students to the types of texts they will most probably encounter beyond and outside the course.

6. How do learners and teachers who have used the materials feel about them? In addition to the previously stated objective questions, it is necessary to gather subjective information in order to gain additional insights into how teachable or learnable the materials really are. This type of information can be gathered via a questionnaire or informal interview.

2.2.3   *The teachers*

When discussing teacher populations, it is again useful to distinguish between natural language and foreign language settings. In a natural setting, teachers usually are native speakers or near-native speakers of the language and can cope with various decision-making steps that deal with language use; on the other hand, in the foreign language setting, teachers are typically non-native speakers who may have never spent time in an English speaking country and therefore may find it much harder to make decisions of a native-like nature.

The teacher population is the most significant factor in determining success of a new syllabus or materials. The attitudes of the teachers and their abilities to adjust to new thinking and what it involves in practical terms are crucial. Therefore, the following factors need to be considered when evaluating the members of the teacher population: (a) the teacher's command of the target language (where it is not the native language), (b) the teacher's training, background, level of higher education, exposure to ideas concerning the nature of language and language learning, teaching experience, and (c) the teacher's attitude towards changes in the program. More can be done in the area of attitudes and training as part of a new program if teacher training is incorporated as a significant component of new materials. On the other hand, the designers have little control in the area of command of the target language. Often this is a given factor which must be taken into account in planning new programs.

Teachers who received traditional training and who have only worked with rather conservative materials may not be equipped professionally or emotionally to handle modern teaching materials which leave a considerable amount of decision making to the teacher. A period of sensitizing may be necessary for both teachers and students before new ideas can be introduced effectively. Often, course designers need to incorporate sensitizing mechanisms into new materials. In order to do that, they need a reliable picture of the teachers who will implement the program.

2.2.4 The learners

The student population is the other significant factor in the classroom. In many new communicative programs, students are expected to take an active part in the learning process. They are put into situations in which they must share responsibilities, make decisions, evaluate their own progress, develop individual preferences, and so on. These requirements may be new and unfamiliar to the students themselves. In order to help them become responsible learners, a period of 'learning how to learn' is vital. Students may have to learn to do group work, to become initiators of activities, etc. In the foreign language setting, students are apt to be of a homogeneous socio-economic background and so the process of sensitizing them to new ways of learning is easier to accomplish. But in the natural language setting, it is more usual for students to come from diverse cultural backgrounds. Thus, they join the language learning classroom with a variety of different assumptions about learning and teaching, a factor which can seriously affect the success of a new program.

2.2.5 *The resources*

Policy-making can be realistic and effective only if it takes into account the limitations of available resources for implementation, both quantitatively and qualitatively. Such limitations on resources can be translated into a number of key factors which need to be considered carefully as part of the policy-making process:

1. Time available for the acquisition of the target language is a key factor and can easily be determined since any planning takes into account the available hours per week, weeks in the school year, and even years for the course. The objectives and the ways in which they can be achieved as always are dependent on the amount of time available and how it is distributed.

2. Classroom setting is also an important factor, reflecting a number of relevant features of the teaching/learning situation. Factors such as the number of students and teachers in the classroom and whether the desks are fixed or easily rearranged might be very important considerations when planning group or individual activities. The actual physical environment of the classroom (light, shape of the room, etc.) is also significant and may affect the learning process positively or negatively. Some of these factors could be altered or made good use of if the language teacher has his/her own classroom but might be serious drawbacks if the teacher has to move from classroom to classroom to give the language lesson.

   Also to be considered is the availability of equipment such as tape recorders, slides, films, pictures, posters, and other such visual and audio features which may greatly affect some of the activities carried out in class. Budgetary restrictions usually mean that ideal planning must be adjusted to realistic limitations.

In planning new programs, it is important to carefully evaluate both existing resources and their limitations since either can render new ideas either feasible or doomed to failure. At times planners might decide to incorporate some of the solutions to these limitations within the new program while at other times it may seem wisest to adjust policy-making to existing reality, possibly even postponing a new program.

2.3 When the materials in use constitute the curriculum and syllabus

So far in our discussion, the program designers' task has been presented from an idealized perspective: a well-planned and carefully conceived program should be based on a thorough analysis of societal patterns of language use. Moreover, changes in existing programs should take place only after a careful study of the instructional plans currently in effect. However, a broadly-based survey of societal language use patterns may be difficult to carry out, except in some abbreviated form. Nevertheless, the program designers utilize whatever information can be collected, always ready to make shifts and adjustments if new information becomes available.

Often, when no curriculum or syllabus exists for a program in operation, the teachers have put together instructional plans based entirely on commercial textbooks. In such cases, the program designers can make use of these materials as sources of vital clues about the existing program. These commercial textbooks, together with interviews and classroom observations, tell the program designer a great deal about decisions which have been made, either implicitly or explicitly, concerning the content of the course. With an understanding of the recent history, shifts, and trends in the field of language pedagogy, the program designers can gather a great many details about the existing program and its underlying approach and goals, simply by carefully studying tables of contents in existing textbooks, teacher's notes, teacher's handbooks, and auxiliary materials.

When the only documents to examine are commercial textbooks in use, the program designers need to be concerned with the following:

1. Do the commercial textbooks in use contain statements about educational and linguistic points of view? Often these appear in an introduction, preface, or in a teacher's guide. Do these policy statements coincide with the views held by the teachers using the materials? Or, are the teachers, themselves, aware of such educational and linguistic orientations?
2. How have the teachers using the textbooks adapted them to the timeframe and other constraints of the course? Some commercial textbooks have scope and sequence charts which indicate the linguistic elements included and the points at which they are introduced in the books.
3. Do the teachers make any cultural adaptations with the textbooks?
   – by changing proper names?
   – by changing place names?
   – by altering culture-bound topics, for example, using local or national holidays, foods, sports, etc., in place of or together with those in the textbooks?
4. Do they see the textbook as serving the goals of their students in terms of examinations to higher levels of education or higher levels in the language program?
5. What adaptations do teachers make to fit local attitudes toward language learning? For example, are conversation sections in the lessons used as dictations or as translation exercises?

2.4   The separate purposes of a curriculum and a syllabus

The course designers' full responsibility is that of setting not only broad, general goals but also specifying objectives which are made accessible to all those involved with the program. The task, of course, is traditionally carried out through written documents which are given any number of different names: guides, plans, outlines, etc. In our discussion, however, two titles are used: curriculum and syllabus.

1. A curriculum contains a broad description of general goals by indicating an overall educational-cultural philosophy which applies across

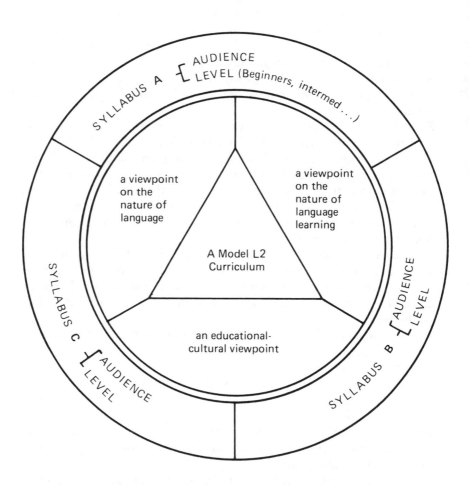

Diagram 2   The relationship of a curriculum to the syllabuses which draw from it

subjects together with a theoretical orientation to language and language learning with respect to the subject matter at hand. A curriculum is often reflective of national and political trends as well.

2. A syllabus is a more detailed and operational statement of teaching and learning elements which translates the philosophy of the curriculum into a series of planned steps leading towards more narrowly defined objectives at each level.

It seems helpful to define a curriculum and a syllabus as separate entities in order to call attention to their particular functions, even though *one* document could contain sections which express the separate purposes. An important reason for differentiating between the two is to stress that a single curriculum can be the basis for developing a variety of specific syllabuses which are concerned with locally defined audiences, particular needs, and intermediate objectives.

2.4.1 The components of a curriculum

Since the curriculum is concerned with a general rationale for formulating policy decisions, it combines educational-cultural goals with language goals. For example, an overall educational approach could focus on one of the following major views: (a) a behavioristic orientation considers the human species to be a passive organism, reacting to external, environmental stimuli; (b) a rational-cognitive orientation considers the human species to be the source and initiator of all acts; (c) a humanistic orientation is concerned with each individual's growth and development, while emphasizing affective factors as well. Culturally, any one of these philosophies may suit a certain community better.

Generally, an educational orientation is compatible with one or more linguistic and language-learning theories. Thus, the behavioristic view is an educational-psychological philosophy which is compatible with a structuralist view of language and a stimulus-response view about human language learning. Diagram 3 shows these three components of an audiolingual curriculum, a view which prevailed in the 1950s and 1960s, as an example of how major views affect the curriculum.

As the theoretical influences on the basis of a language curriculum shifted, the rational cognitive orientation became strongly reflected in the views of human language proposed by transformational-generative linguistics in the 1960s and was associated with the cognitive-code approach to language learning. The humanistic orientation has been closely associated with the communicative view of language. It is the latter that has been the most prominent since the mid-1970s.

It is interesting to trace the genealogy of various well-known views on language teaching. For example, both the grammar-translation approach, which was typically used in teaching Greek and Latin and

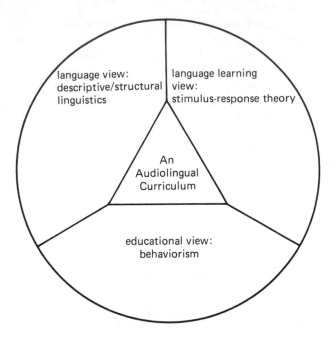

Diagram 3   The components of an audiolingual curriculum

then generalized to modern language teaching, and the much more con-temporary Silent Way approach developed by Gattegno (1972, 1983) have distinct affinities with a rational-cognitive orientation in the way in which they both emphasize the learning of language forms. They do not, however, share a similar view of language learning. While, as an example, the grammar-translation teacher will provide students with lengthy explanations of grammatical points, the Silent Way teacher will provide a model utterance followed by silence which, according to the approach, induces the students to take the initiative for cognitive activi-ties.

   Another contemporary approach which links a rational-cognitive view with a communicative orientation towards language use is the Natural Approach (Krashen and Terrell 1983). This approach has much in com-mon with other contemporary views which emphasize the importance of listening and comprehension at the onset of learning – among them Silent Way. Indeed, the recent Natural Approach has antecedents in a long history of natural methods which have emphasized learning a language through using it rather than by recourse to language analysis. In fact, in the sixteenth century, Michel de Montaigne wrote about his own experiences growing up as a native speaker of Latin, a notion conceived of and carried out by Montaigne's father through strict control of his son's language input (Howatt 1984).

Various other current schools of thought trace their lineages to a humanistic orientation, notably Counseling-Learning (Curran 1972), as well as the beliefs which have grown under the direct influence of Paulo Freire, combining a humanistic view with a particular political view of the world (Wallerstein 1983). Freire developed an educational approach based on his socialist philosophy in which adult learners are encouraged to analyze and challenge the forces in society which keep them passive. The similarities between Freire's approach and Curran's derive from the focus on the students' activist involvement in the learning process.

As indicated in diagram 3, three basic orientations, one concerning language, one concerning language learning, and one concerning pedagogy can be reflected partially or fully in a wide variety of language learning approaches.

2.4.2 Types of syllabuses

In the past decade, a great deal of attention has been paid to the particular language elements that are included in a syllabus and to the organizational system according to which they are presented. Discussions have typically considered the trade-offs, advantages, and disadvantages of three or four major syllabus types: the structural-grammatical syllabus, the semantico-notional syllabus, the functional syllabus, and the situational syllabus.

The familiar structural, grammatical or linguistic syllabus is centered around items such as tenses, articles, singular/plural, complementation, adverbial forms, etc. The notional (or semantico-notional) syllabus came into focus in the early seventies and placed the semantic unit in the center of syllabus organization. Such a syllabus is organized around themes relating to broad areas of meaning such as space, time, obligation, etc. (Wilkins 1976). The functional syllabus, which developed alongside the notional syllabus with various attempts to combine the two, focuses on the social functions of language as the central unit of organization. Thus, a functional syllabus is concerned with elements such as invitations, suggestions, apologies, refusals, etc. (Wilkins 1976; McKay 1980). The fourth type mentioned here, the situational one, although less widespread than some of the others, has probably been known in language learning for hundreds of years with the tourist phrase book as a notable example.

All four of the examples cited (structures, notions, functions and situations) illustrate different realizations of an organizational approach based on discrete units. Recently, however, within the communicative approach to curriculum and syllabus design, the idea of presenting an organizational concept which is not based on separate units but rather on a continuous process of communication and negotiation in the target language has gained in popularity. In this approach, the communicative needs of the learners are the basis on which various linguistic, thematic or functional elements are selected. The role of the teacher is to facilitate the learners' participation in these communicative exchanges. Ideally, there should also be scope for learners to take responsibility to analyze their own needs and accordingly seek help from the teacher or the materials. (The communicative approach is discussed more fully in chapters 4 and 5.)

Course designers who carefully consider the various approaches to syllabus design may arrive at the conclusion that a number of different ones are needed and are best combined in an eclectic manner in order to bring about positive results. Thus, it may be necessary to use a structural/situational syllabus for the first years of a course of study, moving to a functional plan of organization, followed by a notional/skill combination, leading finally to a fully communicative design for the final phases of the course. Such a solution may be suitable for a foreign language setting, while a purely communicative approach might be more applicable in the natural setting. The most important feature of any modern language syllabus, therefore, is its inherent potential for adjustment based on careful decision-making at each level within the course.

Along with seeking out ways to combine various syllabus types, course designers have other considerations. So far in our discussion, the description of syllabus types has been largely based on one dimension – the language content area. In the next chapter, in section 3.2, a framework for building a syllabus around three dimensions rather than only one will be presented.

Practical applications

1. Find a curriculum or syllabus for a course given in an educational setting with which you are familiar. Utilizing that document, evaluate the following: Is the distinction between curriculum and syllabus presented in this chapter valid? If it does not exist in the program that you are examining, would you suggest such a distinction? Are the terminal goals clearly defined? Are there any specifications of the intermediate goals?
2. In terms of the content of the syllabus itself:
   a) How are the items to be taught described? Are they structural elements, language functions, semantic categories, or ...?
   b) Is there obvious continuity of development?

   c) Would a textbook writer be clear about what to focus on in preparing new language materials?
3. In an educational setting in which you are familiar, what information can you gather on the limitation of human and other resources in planning an English language curriculum or syllabus?
4. Select a section of the actual material used in a course and try to answer the questions presented in section 2.2.
5. Find additional commercial textbooks and look at their table of contents for clues about their underlying views on language and language learning. Use the questions in section 2.3 as a model.

References

Celce-Murcia, M. 1980. 'Language teaching methods from the ancient Greeks to Gattegno', *Mextesol Journal* IV(4), pp. 2–13.

Curran, C. A. 1972. *Counseling-learning. A whole person model for education.* New York: Grune and Stratton.

Gattegno, C. 1972. *Teaching foreign languages in schools: The Silent Way.* New York: Education Solutions.

Gattegno, C. 1983. 'The Silent Way'. In J. Oller and R. Amata (Eds.) *Methods That Work.* Rowley, Massachusetts: Newbury House.

Howatt, A. P. R. 1984. *A history of English language teaching.* Oxford: Oxford University Press.

Kelly, L. G. 1969. *25 centuries of language teaching.* Rowley, Massachusetts: Newbury House.

Krashen, S. and T. Terrell. 1983. *The natural approach: language acquisition in the classroom.* San Francisco: Alemany Press, and Oxford: Pergamon Press.

McKay, S. 1980. 'Towards an integrated syllabus'. In K. Croft (Ed.) *Readings in English as a second language*, pp. 72–84. Cambridge, Massachusetts: Winthrop Publishers, Inc.

Wallerstein, N. 1983. *Language and culture in conflict: problem posing in the ESL classroom.* Reading, Massachusetts: Addison-Wesley.

Wilkins, D. A. 1976. *Notional syllabuses.* Oxford: Oxford University Press.

3 How goals become realized through instructional plans

Overview

As this chapter is concerned with the fundamentals of syllabus construction, it deals with the translation of philosophical, theoretical views about language and learning, as shown in diagram 3, into operational goals for instructional plans. The distinction made earlier between a curriculum and a syllabus is further developed in section 3.1, *Translating general goals into syllabus objectives*. A curriculum provides a statement of policy, while a syllabus specifies details of course content.

Section 3.2, *Language content, process, and product in syllabus designs* presents the three basic dimensions of a language syllabus. Content, process, and product are introduced in this chapter and will be further expanded in subsequent chapters since they constitute the three basic components of any instructional plan.

Once the content of the syllabus has been selected, the next step is to select a suitable format. Section 3.3, *Selecting the shape of the syllabus* presents a number of possible formats with examples to illustrate each.

Up to this point, the discussion of course design has been presented independently of methodology. But the issue cannot be avoided. Section 3.4 comes to grips with the question of method: *The place of method* – where do methods belong in comprehensive, instructional planning?

3.1 Translating general goals into syllabus objectives

In chapter 2, section 2.4, it was pointed out that since a curriculum and a syllabus serve separate functions there is benefit in thinking of them as distinct entities. A curriculum deals with abstract, general goals while a syllabus, or the instructional plans, guides teachers and learners in everyday concerns. In fact, a chief task for course designers is to turn abstract curriculum goals into concrete objectives in the syllabus.

3.1.1 A curriculum provides a statement of policy

As also suggested in chapter 2, three broad, abstract areas have an influence on the goals which become articulated through a curriculum,

40

or a statement of policy: a viewpoint on the nature of language, a viewpoint on the nature of language learning, and an educational-cultural philosophy. A position in each one or any of these areas, either directly or indirectly stated, is reflected, in turn, in the formulation of general course goals. For example, the following preface to an adult level ESL course of study serves as a curriculum, or policy statement:

PREFACE

The field of teaching English as a Second Language is a dynamic one that has experienced phenomenal growth and change in the last two decades.

Since their pioneering days as Americanization courses, adult ESL programs have been pacesetters, teaching non-English speaking adults the language necessary for survival in the English-speaking community.

Long before such terms as "communicative competence" and "notional functional syllabus" came into prominence, adult teachers had been helping their students learn to market, to ask their doctors for advice, or to ask for help over the telephone in their daily lessons.

This course outline represents a more formalized approach and design for the teaching of communication skills to adult ESL students. The sample Lesson Plan provides the procedure for presentation and implementation of a communicative lesson.

(from Los Angeles Unified School District 1982 revision. Course outline for English as a second language, levels 1–4. Los Angeles: Adult/Regional Occupational Centers/Program Education Division)

As illustrated by this statement of general goals, designers and planners must always be aware of fluctuations in viewpoints held by linguists towards language, researchers towards language learning, along with the beliefs and values currently held by those in general education circles. In fact, professionalism in course designing, as the example preface illustrates, depends crucially on establishing goals which take into account both specific requirements which meet the program's needs as well as the state of the art in the field of language teaching at a particular point in time.

41

3.1.2   The link between goals and objectives

The connection between general goals at the curriculum level and specific objectives at the syllabus level is evident in the effect which goals have on the three concerns of a syllabus: the dimensions of language content, processes or means, and product or outcomes. In general, curriculum goals tend to place emphasis on one or another of these dimensions.

If a particular theory of language has been adopted as the foundation upon which to write a curriculum, then course designers are apt to ask key questions about language content such as these:

1. What elements, items, units, or themes of language content should be selected for inclusion in the syllabus?
2. In what order or sequence should the elements be presented in the syllabus?
3. What are the criteria for deciding on the order of elements in the syllabus?

On the other hand, if ideas about language learning or a particular philosophy of education have had a strong influence in shaping the course goals, then course planners would necessarily ask questions about the process dimension:

1. How should language be presented to facilitate the acquisition process?
2. What should be the roles of teachers and learners in the learning process?
3. How should the materials contribute to the process of language learning in the classroom?

However, where general goals in terms of specific achievements have played the dominant role in shaping the curriculum, course designers will ask product/outcome questions. For example:

1. What knowledge is the learner expected to attain by the end of the course? What understandings based on analyses of structures and lexis will learners have as an outcome of the course?
2. What specific language skills do learners need in their immediate future, or in their professional lives? How will these skills be presented in the syllabus?
3. What techniques of evaluation or examination in the target language will be used to assess course outcomes?

This linkage is shown graphically in diagram 4: the theoretical and philosophical views which mold the intellectual tone of a curriculum affect how general goals are formed. These general goals, in turn, become the basis for specifying objectives in the three dimensions of a syllabus: language content, processes or means, and product or outcomes.

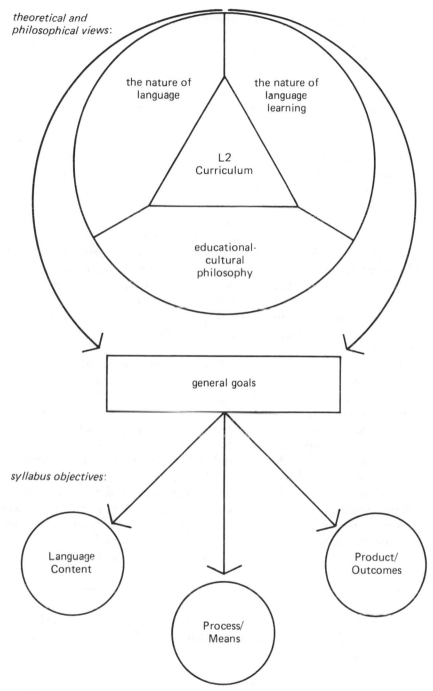

theoretical and philosophical views:

the nature of language

the nature of language learning

L2 Curriculum

educational-cultural philosophy

general goals

syllabus objectives:

Language Content

Process/ Means

Product/ Outcomes

Diagram 4   How goals become instructional objectives

3.1.3 Syllabuses without a curriculum

In the real world, when one looks at language programs in operation, it is possible to find many examples in which a course outline, course of study or some other operational guide on the syllabus level does not contain a statement of more general goals. This type of situation is most common in programs which are not part of a public educational system, either for a community, a state, or a country. However, absence of a concrete statement about policy does not indicate that goals are totally missing. More likely, what it may mean is that the general goals are represented by the beliefs and attitudes of the teachers and administrators in the program, even though there is no written curriculum.

Implicitly held beliefs may be generally shared by all concerned with the operation of the program; it is just that the goals have never been articulated. Or, it could be the case that those in decision-making positions realize that the disparate opinions held by the professional staff could never result in a coherent policy statement since they would be so wide-ranging. In fact, any policy statement that would represent all of the teachers' opinions would have to be extremely general in order not to offend any particular viewpoint. So the program gets along by having various syllabuses which cover specific course objectives to provide direction.

But an absence of a specific policy can result in misunderstandings and misuse of energies. In working out course objectives, for example, if teachers and planners do not agree on basic goals, then discussions can prove frustrating if not fruitless. For example, the basic goal for an academic ESL program at the college level might focus on overall comprehension of spoken English and the ability to read college level texts. These goals could be actualized through organizing sheltered courses in which students improve their English language competence by attending lectures, taking notes, reading required texts, etc. in an academic subject of their interest. The degree of specific instruction necessary in the skills of listening comprehension, note-taking and reading would still need to be worked out at the syllabus level.

On the other hand, it might be established that the general goals are expository writing and advanced library research skills. In such a case, the course syllabus that would be required to carry out these goals would cover quite different content than would the syllabus for overall comprehension of spoken English and the ability to read college level texts. What is needed in this situation are course goals which all concerned can agree upon.

3.2 Language content, process, and product in syllabus designs

Whether or not there is a curriculum which documents the underlying goals, language programs tend to vary according to whether they stress (a) language content, or the specific matter to be included; (b) process, or the manner in which language content is learned; (c) product, or outcomes such as the language skills learners are expected to master. Attention to all three dimensions, of course, is vital. However, in the history of language pedagogy shifting views on the nature of language and the nature of language learning have tended to make one or another more prominent. In turn, language courses have reflected these shifts in focus. In this section these three dimensions are discussed and illustrated in light of how each has played a role in language teaching during the recent history of the field.

3.2.1 The language content dimension

Content has traditionally included three important subcomponents. Along with language content, or structures, grammatical forms, etc., familiar to all, language courses have included thematic and situational content as well. Thematic content refers to the topics of interest and areas of subject knowledge selected as themes to talk or read about in order to learn and use the target language. In selecting appropriate themes, one would draw on considerations of learners' age and other social criteria. In the academic setting, their need for subject area knowledge and other school objectives could be addressed. Sometimes the situational and/or linguistic subcomponents carry higher priority so the choice of theme becomes secondary over other considerations.

Situational content refers to the context within which the theme and the linguistic topics are presented; for example, the place, time, type of interaction, and the participants that are presented in the learning situation. These might involve shopping for some specific item in a department store as the place: the participants enact the roles of a customer and salesperson. In a syllabus or materials which emphasize the importance of situation selection, there would be a list of useful situations which learners would encounter during the course; the other elements such as structures and vocabulary would be selected to fit this list of useful, functional situations.

But in traditional syllabuses and materials, more often than not both situation and thematic considerations have been overridden by the linguistic content. In turn, the linguistic content has been determined by a particular theoretical view of the nature of language. For example, if the linguistic content is primary, then the thematic and situational content are usually selected after the linguistic content has been established. Their main function is supportive and complementary to the linguistic topic.

In the audiolingual approach, which drew from both structuralism in linguistics and behaviorism in psychology, emphasis was placed on careful sequencing of grammatical structures and on strict control of the presentation of vocabulary at the initial stages. As a result, the situational and the thematic content were dictated by the structures and vocabulary items introduced in each lesson. This factor was so powerful that often the thematic content was completely ignored and the grammar and vocabulary presented in isolated and unrelated sentences without any thematic thread.

3.2.2   The process dimension

As used in syllabus development, process refers to how instruction is carried out and learning is achieved. To describe process within the learning context is to describe the learners' behavior and the activities in which they are involved while learning is going on. Process results from three major areas:

1. The organization of the language content which brings about certain activities.
2. The roles that teachers and learners take on during the learning process.
3. The types of activities and tasks in which learners are engaged.

All approaches to language learning have placed some degree of emphasis on process, but each viewed the concept of process differently. Thus, the audiolingual approach singled out pattern-practice leading to automatic use as the most important feature of process. The cognitive-code approach focused on hypothesis testing and the creative use of language as key features of process. More recently, the communicative approach to language teaching has placed a much higher premium on process than ever before and process is now viewed as aiming at cognitively and communicatively engaging activities of as wide a variety as possible. Process in the syllabus is, therefore, highly affected by views of language learning and educational concepts in general.

I   ORGANIZATION

Decisions relating to the organization of course content, the presentation of new topics, and their sequence and scope of treatment, all depend on the underlying educational and linguistic assumptions as well as on our concurrent understanding of the learning process. Linguistic approaches usually view language as made up of discrete units such as words, sentences, patterns or functions. The discrete unit fits well with a carefully planned series of steps. Learners are expected to master the particular unit of work before they continue to the next one since even the process, according to this approach, is viewed as consisting of distinct points of mastery along the continuum. Moreover, some learning theories advocate a sequence which progresses from simple to complex forms, while others begin with the most frequently used forms and advance to less frequent ones. At times the decisive factor is the functional load of the form, or its usefulness in real-life situations and contexts. According to this view, learners should encounter the more common forms earlier so as to ensure effective learning.

Organization can be viewed in two ways: as it relates to an overall program, and as it concerns presentation of new topics. Within a program, content can be organized in a variety of ways as described in section 3.3. The most familiar shape or system of organization is sequential ordering of elements, aptly called 'a linear table of contents', since the items to be taught or the areas covered are set out as in a line. However, the order in which linguistic elements (units of grammar) are traditionally presented in beginning-level English language textbooks apparently has no theoretical justification. Rather, 'it is the embodiment of the cumulative experience of language teachers' (Alexander 1976). As an example, consider the fact that most textbooks of the structural type start out with 'be' sentences. One could claim that 'be' sentences are highly productive in English, but beyond that there is no sound theoretical reason why, according to structural theories, a syllabus should begin with 'be' rather than with some other sentence type.

The second feature of organization relates to the presentation of new learning items. Some views advocate strict adherence to an inductive approach, where examples are given first leading towards generalization; others hold out for a deductive one, where the rule is given first and then applied to various examples, while still others combine the two or alternatively attach no importance to whether an inductive or a deductive presentation is used. The choice among these different variants of presentation depends on the perception one has of the acquisition process. Audiolingualism called for an inductive presentation, while both the cognitive-code and communicative approaches maintain that some students may learn more successfully through inductive modes while others will be more suited to deductive – or, there is no single right way.

2   THE ROLE OF THE TEACHER

In a relatively brief period of time, the teacher's role in the language class has shifted markedly. In the grammar-translation tradition, language teachers were thought of as people who knew the target language and its literature thoroughly, but did not necessarily speak the language fluently. The textbook contained all the necessary information about the language; the teacher's assignment was to be a faithful implementor by explaining its contents.

Then, during audiolingualism the role of the teacher changed radically. Now the teacher had to be a near-native speaker of the target language in order to serve as a model for learners while conducting oral repetition drills with the whole class or groups. Emphasis was on the performance during the lesson itself, so the teacher did relatively minimal preparation in the analysis of language content. The textbook provided all the necessary material for classroom work.

Within cognitive-code theories, the teacher facilitates while students refine their control of the target language, often through the strategy of hypothesis testing. The teacher is expected to have good general proficiency of both target and native language in order to both analyze and explain difficulties as they occur. Teachers are expected to be expert observers in order to point out and make use of their learners' various learning and cognitive styles, guiding them to suitable language activities.

Affective/humanistic attitudes towards language learning have expanded the role of the teacher/facilitator in many directions. The teacher plays additional roles: as a resource person who provides students with materials beyond the textbook and as an evaluator, matching learners' needs with those set out in the program or curriculum in order to bring the two closer together. (See chapter 4, section 4.4.)

3   THE ROLE OF THE LEARNER

Similarly, learners' roles have taken on different dimensions during various periods. The grammar-translation tradition enabled learners to develop their own learning techniques, focusing mainly on the knowledge that was acquired about the target language and its literature. Students read, wrote, translated, and memorized texts. Those who managed to develop their own successful techniques acquired a good academic command of the language.

The audiolingual view creates robot-like learners who, within the theory, are expected to carry out mechanical manipulations in order to form habits which are expected to lead them to fluency in the target language. Individuals take little responsibility except for participating in choral activities followed by controlled writing practice. Basically, students are spoon-fed and carefully led from one step to the next with minimal room for failure, error, or experimentation.

In cognitive-code practices, learners are expected to internalize linguistic rules which in turn will help them use the language on their own. Learners are given choices regarding types of activities, amount of practice, and the language skill or medium in which the activity is carried out.

Drawing on humanistic-affective educational philosophies, communicative goals have further increased the learners' role by encouraging them to share responsibility for various elements: the learning process, the content, and the outcomes. Since communicative aspects of interaction in the target language are emphasized, students must learn to function effectively in pairs and small groups, sometimes teaching each other, at other times discovering answers to problems together.

The type of activities or tasks students carry out is a natural outcome of the degree of control maintained by both teacher and textbook, as well as the level of student involvement. Approaches which favor considerable control on the part of the teacher and the textbook result in an abundance of mechanical and predictable tasks which leave very little room for error or for learners' initiative. Approaches which favor a communicative-humanistic view usually present learners with ample opportunities for unpredictable and negotiable outcomes to activities.

3.2.3 The product dimension

Product in syllabus design refers to the specification of the expected outcomes of a course of study. These specifications are used by various groups in quite different ways. Resource agencies who commission new courses and planners who propose them describe the anticipated outcomes in order to justify costs, highlight benefits, or both, while a policy-making authority uses such specifications to assess the usefulness of the courses for the intended learner population.

Specification of course outcomes ideally should be linked to a careful evaluation of the audience's needs for the target language. Publishers often initiate the process of materials development with a survey of the field and from their findings define the goals of a new course. In this case, the publisher's specifications serve as the basis for writers. A determination of course objectives, therefore, is important for the educational authorities who intend to adopt a course, for the potential learners who need to decide whether to join this or that course, and for the writers who will develop the actual materials to achieve the expected outcomes.

Course outcomes can be divided into knowledge-oriented or skill-oriented types. When course planners choose to focus on the knowledge aspect of the course product, they must list the elements of content that learners are expected to master. Basically, a content/knowledge-oriented statement of outcomes will answer the question: *what* are learners expected to *know* by the end of the course? Content can be specified as actual reading selections to be covered during the course, as linguistic structures or functions, as vocabulary – defined both quantitatively and qualitatively – or it can be specified in terms of all these areas of content.

Focus on knowledge has been associated with emphasis on accuracy in language courses since learners are expected to become proficient in linguistic forms. This approach is compatible with a viewpoint of language which emphasizes discrete points of grammar; the students' mastery can be exhibited on a discrete point test. This type of test attempts to answer the question, what do the students know with respect to specific areas of content which were stated as syllabus objectives?

When course designers choose to focus on skills rather than on knowledge or content, the definition of product is much more closely related to the actual use learners are expected to make of the new language. Skill specification must be based on a careful survey and evaluation of the needs of a particular student population in terms of present and future expectations. If the students plan to use the target language in order to read academic or technical material, for example, then the product should reflect this by stating the specific reading skills they need to be proficient in by the end of the course; skimming, scanning, reading with comprehension at a certain rate of speed, etc. If the immediate needs of the student population are to communicate orally with native speakers of the target language, then the outcomes of the course would focus on oral communication skills with this objective stated as specific types of interaction: to be able to communicate in an oral job interview, in a patient/doctor interview, etc.

There is a significant difference between a knowledge-oriented approach and a skill-oriented approach since the former is less sensitive to specific needs and is, therefore, more easily adaptable to any population of learners. The latter, the skill-oriented approach, inherently focuses on more carefully defined, individual needs for language use. A further significant difference between knowledge/content and skill-oriented goals is the fact that content can be divided more easily into interim objectives to be attained at various points during the course. On the other hand, skill mastery is more difficult to break up into interim objectives. Yet, short-term or interim objectives are important for course planning since they guide the writers in selecting content and procedures, allowing for the development of measurement techniques to evaluate achievement.

3.3   Selecting the shape of the syllabus

The basic dilemma which course planners must reconcile is that language is infinite, but a syllabus must be finite. Moreover, this finite or selected content requires some kind of organization, or format in a shape which is best suited to the particular project's objectives. In this section, five possible types are briefly discussed and illustrated.

3.3.1   The linear format

The format traditionally adopted for discrete element content, particularly grammar or structures, is the linear shape. When designers utilize it, issues of sequencing and grading are of paramount importance. Linguistic and pedagogical principles determine the order in which items will be presented. Once the sequence has been determined, internal grading of each unit and among units follows from it, resulting in an organization which must be maintained in its original format. In other words, teachers cannot change the order of units or skip some without upsetting the careful grading which has been embedded in the sequence.

However, a strict linear shape does not work well when the categories of language content are notional or functional since there is no inherent sequence or order in them which seems best (Johnson 1982). Many textbooks use linear shapes although without employing the principles of ordering.

Illustration 3.1 shows part of a table of contents of a beginning level textbook, *English Alpha* (Units 1–7), in which linear ordering of grammatical elements follows a familiar outline. The 'communication practice' in each unit in which various language functions are introduced appears to be related in some way to the grammar base. However, no rationale is given for the selection of particular functional categories either in the students' book or the teacher's edition. Moreover, listed in the lessons themselves as 'goals', they appear as 'personal goals', for example 'asking for information' in Unit 2, 'problem solving goals', for example 'guessing what it is' in Unit 3 and 'situational goals', for example 'going to the post office' in Unit 3. (The issue of integrating grammatical and functional aspects in a syllabus is discussed in considerable detail in chapters 5 and 6.)   ⟫→

3 How goals become realized through instructional plans

Illustration 3.1

Contents

3.3.2   The modular format

Well suited to courses which integrate thematic or situational language content with a skills orientation regarding the course outcomes, a modular format is often used for a syllabus designed for a program in which the objective is maximum flexibility in the materials to be used. Since it often turns out to be bulky, modular organization is better suited to the space in a file cabinet than between the two covers of a textbook.

Illustration 3.2 is taken from the Instructor's Handbook of a university level course which follows a modular plan in which academically-oriented skills and thematic units are integrated. Each module, consisting

Illustration 3.2   Thematic/modular

The topics available for weeks 6–14 are:

Culture Shock

Mobility and Its Effects on Society

Issues in American Media (especially TV)

Social Change

Relationships and the Family

Crime and Punishment

Corporate Responsibility

The Future and Our Values

Keeping Fit

Week 1	Weeks 2–5	Weeks 6–14	Week 15
Diagnostic Week: 'Levels of Language'	Student Orientation: 'American Education'	Regular Unit Presentations: Teacher and students select from above list of topics	Final Examinations: Teacher selects from above, one which has not been used during semester.

(from American Language Institute, University of Southern California Instructor's Handbook for Intermediate Academic English: 201. 1982, by Mary Alvin and Cheryl Kraft) of a sequence of skill-building tasks, is carried out during a 2–3 week period, maintaining the same unit theme throughout:

1. Reading: students do background reading as preparation for the lecture.
2. Listening comprehension/note-taking: students hear a mini-lecture (25 minutes) presented by their instructor and take notes.
3. Reading/writing: students use their notes to prepare for a quiz.
4. Reading: students read about the unit theme from a variety of sources.
5. Speaking: students engage in panel discussions, solve problems in small groups, give prepared talks, etc.
6. Writing: students write 500-word essays on topics related to the thematic unit. Writing proceeds from brainstorming, to outlining, and through first and second drafts.

Illustration 3.2 shows a semester plan which lists the thematic units from which students and their instructor can select. Thus, during weeks 6–14, a typical class would work on three topics, but each time the same cycle of skills is repeated. The integration of the skills cycle and the thematic unit constitutes a module.

3.3.3 The cyclical format

This is an organizational principle which enables teachers and learners to work with the same topic more than once, but each time a particular one reappears it is at a more complex or difficult level. However, the criteria for determining what more difficult areas of a grammatical structure might be relies on an experienced writer/teacher's experience. In the cyclical shape, the concept is that new subject matter should not be introduced once in a syllabus and then dropped; rather, it should be reintroduced in different manifestations at various times in the course.

In *English in situations* (O'Neill 1970) the same grammatical topics which are reintroduced in Part A are recycled in Parts B and C.

Illustration 3.3

CONCEPTS	UNIT	PART A
PRESENT SIMPLE vs. PRESENT CONTINUOUS	1	'They do' vs. 'They are doing.' Position of 'often' 'never' etc.
MASS AND UNIT	2	'How much' vs. 'How many' 'There is/are a lot of . . .' 'There is/are' vs. 'they are/it is.'
FUTURE AND IMPERATIVE	3	'Going to do' 'Do!' and 'Don't do!'
PAST SIMPLE, CONTINUOUS, PERFECT AND FUTURE IN THE PAST	4	'Walk/walked' etc. and 'Get/got' 'Did he . . .?' and 'He didn't' 'Was/were' and 'What . . . like?' vs. 'How . . .?' 'used to do/be/have
ADJECTIVES AND ADVERBS	5	Adjectives vs. Adverbs 'as . . . as' vs. '. . .er than' 'better' and 'worse'
PRESENT PERFECT CONTRASTED WITH OTHER TENSES	6	'did something . . . ago' 'has been/had for . . .' and 'has been doing for . . .' 'since' vs. 'for'
SPECIAL PROBLEMS OF WORD ORDER AND MODALS	7	'say'/'said' with reported speech 'tell someone something' 'could you tell me the way to . . .?'
VERB PLUS OBJECT PLUS INFINITIVE AND RELATED MODALS	8	'Would you . . .?' and 'May I . . .' 'tell someone to do . . .', and 'ask someone to do . . .' 'tell/ask/show someone how to . . .'
GERUNDS	9	hate/stop/enjoy/remember doing simple revision of 'who, 'which', and 'that' . . .
CONDITIONALS AND MODALS OF SUGGESTION ETC.	10	'Shall I . . .?' 'Shall we . . .?' 'Would you like to?' 'Would you like a . . .?' 'I'd like a', and 'I'd like to.'
PASSIVE REFLEXIVE AND RELATED CONSTRUCTIONS	11	'hurt himself' etc. (reflexives) 'wash', 'dress', 'feel.' (Non-reflexive) 'themselves/ourselves' vs. 'each other'

(from *English in situations* by Robert O'Neill © Oxford University Press 1970)

PART B	PART C
'is/are doing' in the future 'has/have' vs. 'is/are having'	'always does' vs. 'is always doing' 'should/can/must do' vs. 'should/can/must be doing'
'some' vs. 'any' 'very few' vs. 'very little' 'go to church/school/prison etc.' vs. 'go to THE church/school etc.'	Use and omission of definite article with concrete and abstract nouns words like 'news' etc. that never take 'a'
'I'll do it . . .' (willingness) 'I'll do it before/if/when/as soon as something happens'	'Will do until' vs. 'will have done by' 'Will do' vs. 'will be doing' 'might do' and 'might be doing' in future
'Was/were doing' vs. 'did' 'while' vs. 'during' 'during' vs. 'for'	'had done' vs. 'did' 'had no idea something was going to happen'
Position of 'very much' and 'very often' after object 'fast and hard' 'hardly/hardly (anything) at all, 'hardly ever' 'embarrassed/embarrassing'	'look/sound' etc. with adjective 'look/feel good' vs. 'look well' 'should have done' vs. 'should have been doing'
'has/have been' vs. 'was were' 'have you ever?' 'have you done that yet?' 'did it for' vs. 'has been doing it for . . .' 'It's the . . . est I've ever . . .'	'has been doing' vs. 'has done' 'had been doing' vs. 'did' 'has been' vs. 'did'
'What are you looking at?' 'What did you do that for?' 'Who/what did . . .?' 'explain something to somebody'	'supposed to do/be doing/have done' "Who knows Mary" etc. vs. "Who does Mary know?" "Isn't tall enough to dance with" etc.
'want someone to do' 'doesn't/didn't want someone to do' 'mustn't vs. 'don't/doesn't have to' 'Don't you think you should . . .?'	'make someone do' vs. 'let someone do' 'get someone to do' 'will/won't be able to do' and 'will have to do'
'stop/remember doing' 'stop remember to do' 'by/for/of doing'	Verb plus Object plus Preposition plus Gerund Patterns ('stop him from doing' etc.) 'try doing' vs. 'try to do' 'difficulty in doing' etc.
'would/wouldn't do if I were you.' 'would do if did/didn't' 'wish plus would do/were/had/did'	'It's time someone did' 'Would have done if had done.' 'wish had done.'
'has/have been done' 'have something done' 'has been done' vs. 'was done'	'Is being done' 'Might/needn't/should have been done' had (experienced) something done.'

3.3.4   The matrix format

As a shape which gives users maximum flexibility to select topics from a table of contents in a random order, the matrix is well suited to situational content. In *It's time to talk* (Dubin and Margol 1977) six cate-

Illustration 3.4   OVERALL PLAN

COMMUNICATION TASKS	chapter 1 strategies in the classroom	chapter 2 places in the community	chapter 3 services in the community
share and tell	lesson 1 Giving 　Introductions Mixers Who Am I? Papers, Scissors, 　Stone Waist Wagers Follow the Leader	lesson 7 Ice Cream 　Concoctions Hangouts A Good Place to 　Eat A Place for 　Everyone and 　Everything Places of Worship	lesson 13 Playing the 　Numbers Traveler's Aid See My Lawyer Recycling 　Reminders City Life
interviews, polls, interactions	lesson 2 It Takes Two Talk About Taste Day and Night Interviewing 　Famous People The Roving 　Reporter	lesson 8 Get to Know Your 　Auto Shop Let's Have Lunch Is Health Food 　Healthier? The Supermarket 　Poll Living Quarters The Animal 　Shelter	lesson 14 Registering to 　Vote Mail Service Continuing 　Education Youth Groups The More the 　Better? Too Many Cars
treasure hunts	lesson 3 May I Have Your 　Autograph? Locating 　Landmarks Twenty Questions Finding Ads Good and Bad 　Omens	lesson 9 Recreation 　Centers Fascinating 　Exhibits Bargain Basements Getting a Library 　Card Secret 　Destinations Drug Informa- 　tion Centers	lesson 15 Directory 　Assistance House Hunting You Can Bank 　on It The Yellow Pages Telephone Talk Melting Pot Versus 　Salad Bowl

gories of tasks intersect in the matrix with six situational settings. The resulting squares of the matrix each include four or five communicative activities which incorporate the given tasks with the particular situation or setting.

chapter 4 people in the community	chapter 5 media in the community	chapter 6 family and fun

lesson 19
 	
Movie Stars
The Best Teacher
  I Ever Had
Salespeople and
  Shoppers
A Do-It-Yourself
  Person
Positive and
  Negative People
Paramedics
	lesson 25
	
	Musical Choices
	Favorite Films
	Dear _____, I
	  Have a Problem
	Read All About It
	If I Had Enough
	  Time
		lesson 31
		
		Riding
		Amusement Parks
		The Family Circle
		The Holiday Spirit
		Do-It-Yourself
		  Sports
		Spectator Sports

lesson 20
 	
Smokers
Parents
A Police Officer's
  Duties
Antique Dealers
  and Junk
  Collectors
Good Conversa-
  tionalists
	lesson 26
	
	Goings On
	See You in the
	  Funny Papers
	Cover Stories
	T-Shirt Talk
	Sensational News
	The Press
	  Conference
		lesson 32
		
		Where Do You
		  Come From?
		Pets
		Hobbies
		How Others Live
		Senior Citizens

lesson 21
 	
Know Your
  Neighbor
Eaters
Plant Lovers
Handy People
Gourmet Cooks
	lesson 27
	
	What's Playing
	  Tonight?
	Freebees
	Look up the
	  Program
	Guess the Product
	Looking for
	  Messages
	Buy, Sell, Rent,
	  or Trade
		lesson 33
		
		Family Photos
		The Doctor's
		  Office
		Homemade
		  Holidays
		Getting A Driver's
		  License
		On a Diet?

⟫→

3   How goals become realized through instructional plans

COMMUNICATION TASKS	chapter 1 strategies in the classroom	chapter 2 places in the community	chapter 3 services in the community
asking for information	lesson 4 Unknown Identities What Am I Holding? Chain Questions Categories Body Language	lesson 10 Bumper Stickers Out-of-Town Visitors Garage Sales Campsites The Fire Station Exploring Neighborhoods	lesson 16 Do You Have the Time? Everybody Talks About It Asking for Help Postal Rates and Regulations Community Health Care
discussions, panels, debates	lesson 5 I Can Read You Like a Book Burning Issues Newsmaker Panels To Tell the Truth The Clothes People Wear Natural Disasters	lesson 11 Favorite Cities The No-Smoking Section In-Groups and Out-Groups The Suggestion Box Talking on a Soapbox	lesson 17 Shopping Knowhow Buying on Credit From the Cradle to the Grave Bilingual Education Your Money's Worth
creating stories	lesson 6 New Looks for Old What's New? Group Stories My Friend _____ Word Plays A Dark, Stormy Night	lesson 12 Travel Talk The Shop on _____ Street What Would You Do If . . . ? Tourist Traps Fantasy in Art	lesson 18 The Way of Life May I Have an Appointment If I Were the Mayor Friendly Advice Timetables

chapter 4 people in the community	chapter 5 media in the community	chapter 6 family and fun
lesson 22 Get Fit Your Astrological Sign Tuning In to Children The Expressions People Use Who Calls Who What?	lesson 28 What Happened Today? A Little Bit of _____ Talk Shows Alternative Media In the Air	lesson 34 A Family Trip Head of the Household Party Invitations My Family Tree Luxuries Teach a Child
lesson 23 Liberated Women Married People/ Divorced People Single Parents Educated People Petitioners Spoiled Brats	lesson 29 Film Fans TV Around the World What Makes You Laugh? The Sounds in the Air X-Rated Movies	lesson 35 What's a Friend? Sibling Rivalry How Do You See Your Parents? When My Kids Grow Up An Ethical Dilemma
lesson 24 Who Do People Live With? A Blind Walk People Who Want to . . . Handicapped People Imagine that You Are Famous	lesson 30 Classified Ad Categories Far Out Letters to the Editor Ad-Lib Scenes Quiz Kids	lesson 36 I'd Like to Be a . . . Earning Money Fables, Myths, and Tales Emotions I'd Rather . . .

Fraida Dubin, Myrna Margol, *It's Time To Talk*; Communication Activities for Learning English as a New Language © 1977. Reprinted by permission of Prentice-Hall, Englewood Cliffs, New Jersey

3.3.5 The story-line format

The issue of maintaining coherence in a syllabus built on notions and functions was brought up by Wilkins (1976:66). His suggestion that the introduction of a story-line might 'have the effect of ensuring thematic continuity and of helping to resolve questions of the ordering of categories in relation to one another' has been taken up by various textbook writers: For example, Griffin in *Follow me to San Francisco* (1981) and

3 How goals become realized through instructional plans

Abbs, Ayton and Freebairn in *Strategies* (1975). The story-line format, since it is basically a narrative, is of a different type than the ones illustrated above. Further, it could be used in conjunction with any of them.

Illustration 3.5

Contents

Brian Abbs, Angela Ayton and Ingrid Freebairn, *Strategies* © 1975, Longman Group Limited

62

Illustration 3.6

Contents

Suzanne Griffin, *Follow me to San Francisco* © 1981, BBC English by Radio and Television

3.4   The place of method

What is the place of method in course designing? Should a particular method be a focal element around which a syllabus is developed? Whether the assignment is designing programs for others or providing instruction directly to students, conventional wisdom suggests that so-called 'methods' should be an essential element. However, in professional curriculum and syllabus designing, the need for incorporating so-called methods simply disappears because their function has been carried out through the specifications in the instructional plans and materials. The method – however one defines it – is *in* the curriculum, syllabus, and materials. This does not mean, of course, that methodology for teachers or attention to classroom practices of various kinds is being discarded; but this area is not at the center of interest in this discussion.

The most clear-cut definition of methods, and one that became widely adopted in the field, was offered by Anthony (1963). In the context of audiolingualism which prevailed at that time, he explained method in relation to two other terms, approach and techniques. Approach took in both theoretical views of language along with psychological ones relating to the learner. Thus, reflecting his times, for Anthony approach subsumed a structural or descriptive linguistics paradigm of language and a stimulus-response theory of language learning.

In a model which worked as a flowchart, method, in turn, included 'the selection of materials to be taught, the gradation of these materials, their presentation and pedagogical implementation to induce learning.' Techniques were everyday classroom practices and procedures. While this definition of method carried out some of the functions of both a syllabus and materials, the definition did not include the syllabus's role of specifying what language content is to be included. However, Anthony's model worked quite efficiently, for the view of language content which was assumed in audiolingual terms was solely grammatical. So, one could say that in Anthony's frame of reference, his definitions were viable.

Recently, methods seem to have exploded in all directions, to such an extent that the term name-methods, like name-brands, can be used to describe them. Everything is called a method, whether or not it fits Anthony's definition. One element these name-methods have in common is that they tend to be concerned with partial segments of the whole spectrum. Some are strongly focused on one aspect of the basis for a curriculum, namely the nature of the language learner, others are grounded in particular educational philosophies (Richards 1984).

Influenced by psycholinguistics, those methods that are language-learner oriented address the question: What is the nature of second language learning and what is the nature of the second language learner? So, for example, methods such as Silent Way, Total Physical Response, Suggestopedia, and Natural Approach are all based on hypotheses about psychological aspects of language learning. Others, notably Community Language Learning, are concerned with particular philosophies of education.

It is important to note that these psychologically-based name-methods tend not to address themselves in a serious way to questions about language content or the vital *what* aspect of the syllabus. Nor are they very much concerned with the socio-cultural setting of language teaching and learning. A program designer relying on one of the name-methods mentioned above as the exclusive basis for a curriculum would need to fill in a great deal of the big picture, along with most of the details.

The name-methods which have been cited differ among themselves in the amount of attention they pay to techniques. However, many other so-called methods are essentially techniques through and through. They offer suggestions for classroom activities – what to do tomorrow morning. Very often they are ideas that teachers have found to be successful in their own classrooms. Typically, their authors do not concern themselves with what applicability or appropriateness the techniques may hold for differing audiences of teachers/learners in various instructional settings. The task of adaptation is left to the program designer who chooses to incorporate the ideas into materials.

For professionals who are concerned with program design, an important limitation of prevailing name and lesser-known methods is their restricted scope. Those that concentrate on the nature of the language learner may offer interesting insights, but generally fail to provide a rich enough field from which to fully articulate goals for a language program. Those that are solely techniques, by calling themselves methods are simply lambs masquerading in sheep's clothing.

In other ways, the perspective of the name-methods is basically out of harmony with the intent of professional program designing which begins by assessing the total context in which instructional plans are formulated. Name-methods, by contrast, are concerned with providing individual teachers with answers to most if not all questions. They tend to offer well-developed rationales, or sets of beliefs, for those who are ready to accept and work within a fairly closed system. In effect, the belief system or name-method moves from its guru to the disciple, or as expressed by Maley (1983:79) 'the approach gathers around it a ritual set of procedures, a priesthood (complete with the initiatory courses necessary to license practice) and a body of holy writ and commentary.'

The result turns out to be an emphasis on virtuoso teaching, with all of the wisdom lying in a single teacher's head – the person who was instructed in the name-method or who was brought into the fold. Often, there is little recorded on paper – no developed curriculum, syllabus, or materials for others to use who will next have the same teaching assignment. An obvious result is that rugged individualism can prevail over cooperation and team-effort.

Along with emphasizing the individual teacher rather than programs, courses, or societal, cultural and educational goals, name-methods seem to see all teachers as the same. There is little attention to the profound differences between native speaker and non-native speaker teachers or, in an ESL setting, between language teachers and experienced teachers who are new to teaching a language, particularly one which they know as a native. In effect, with name-methods all true-believers who care to join are welcome.

In spite of these drawbacks, the name-methods have served the field of language pedagogy because of their orientation towards using language for communicative purposes. As bridges between mechanistic, audiolingual practices and recent expanded views of content, process, and product, their serious impact and influence must be noted. In many ways, they stand as important stepping stones to more fully rounded views which have come to be known as communicative language teaching.

Practical applications

1. Examine in detail the syllabus for a course or program with which you are familiar. Find out:
   a) What elements of language content are specified?
   b) What course outcomes or objectives in terms of specific achievements are stated?
   c) What processes are suggested for actual classroom activities?
2. Try to find other examples of syllabus shapes in either published textbooks or in a course curriculum or syllabus. Share your findings with the group.
3. Interview a colleague who has participated in a workshop or training session for one of the name-methods listed in section 3.4. Prepare for the interview by formulating a list of questions. You may want to adapt those listed in section 3.1.2 which describe the dimensions of language content, processes/means and product/outcomes. Find out how the name-method in question deals with each of these three dimensions.

References

Abbs, B., A. Ayton and I. Freebairn. 1975. *Strategies.* London: Longman.
Alexander, L. G. 1976. 'Where do we go from here? A reconsideration of some basic assumptions affecting course design'. *English Language Teaching* 30:(2), pp. 89–103.
Alvin, M. and C. Kraft. 1982. *Instructor's Handbook for Intermediate Academic English: 201.* Los Angeles: American Language Institute, USC.
Anthony, E. M. 1963. 'Approach, method, and technique'. *English Language Teaching* 17 (January), pp. 63–7. (Reprinted in H. B. Allen and R. N. Campbell, (Eds.) *Teaching English as a second language,* second edition, 1972. New York: McGraw-Hill, Inc.)
Dubin, F. and M. Margol. 1977. *It's time to talk.* Englewood Cliffs: Prentice Hall.
Griffin, S. 1981. *Follow me to San Francisco.* New York: Longman Inc. and London: BBC English by Radio and Television.

Johnson, K. 1982. *Communicative syllabus design and methodology*. Oxford: Pergamon Press.

Los Angeles Unified School District 1982 revision. *Course outline for English as a second language, levels 1–4*. Los Angeles: Adult/Regional Occupational Centers/Program Education Division.

Maley, A. 1983. 'I got religion! Evangelism in TEFL'. In M. Clarke and J. Handscombe (Eds.) *On TESOL '82: Pacific perspectives on language learning and teaching*. Washington D.C.: TESOL.

O'Neill, R. 1970. *English in situations*. London: Oxford University Press.

Richards, J. C. 1984. 'The secret life of methods'. *TESOL Quarterly*: 18:1.

Sutherland, K. (Ed.) 1980. *English Alpha*. Boston, Massachusetts: Houghton Mifflin Co.

Wilkins, D. A. 1976. *Notional syllabuses*. Oxford: Oxford University Press.

4   A curriculum developed on communicative goals

Overview

In chapter 4, the theoretical background for a communicative curriculum is traced by pointing out its origins in the areas which provide a curriculum with its foundation. Utilizing the model for a language course curriculum (chapter 2) – or an idealized curriculum – a communicative curriculum draws from three major areas: a view of the nature of language as seen by the field of sociolinguistics, a cognitively based view of language learning, and a humanistic approach in education. These theoretical views which influence the goals of a communicative curriculum are shown in diagram 5.

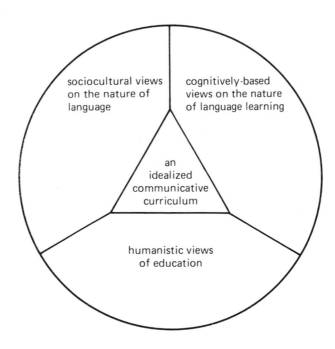

Diagram 5   An idealized communicative curriculum: the theoretical views which influence it

No matter how one defines communicative language teaching, it has emerged as a prevailing point of view as attested by its widespread use in book titles, conference papers, and lectures. But as with the tale about the five blind men who touched separate parts of an elephant and so each described something else, the word 'communicative' has been applied so broadly that it has come to have different meanings for different people.

For program designers, planning for communicative goals calls for adopting a distinct point of view. In the concrete terms in which planners must think and work, it means drawing on ideas which are quite different from those that influenced either cognitive-code or audiolingual based courses. It means distinct underlying attitudes towards the nature of language, the nature of language learning, and the educational framework in which language programs take place. Communicative goals may not serve all language programs appropriately. It is up to the designers of a curriculum to make that decision; but it is one that should be made only by those who have an understanding of what communicative goals imply.

4.1 Sociocultural views of the nature of language

The outlook of sociolinguistics provides the theoretical perspective on language for communicative curriculum designs. Sociolinguistics views any language as inseparable from its sociocultural context. Therefore, most of the theoretical work in sociolinguistics has been directed towards constructing hypotheses concerning the nature of this connection between language and society or culture. Though it gained prominence in the 1960s and 1970s as a dynamic, interdisciplinary field, actually the roots of sociolinguistics go back many generations. In the United States, its antecedents were social anthropologists such as Sapir and Whorf who, in the 1920s and 1930s, were concerned with the relationship of meaning in culture and language. In Britain, Malinowski, Firth, and more recently Halliday built theoretical models which encompassed elements in language with factors in the social and cultural matrix in which language is grounded. Before World War II, the Prague school of linguistics studied the sociocultural context of written texts.

A central concern to linguists who study language in its social context is the phenomenon of variation at all structural levels. Rather than to put differences in language performances aside as many linguists have, sociolinguists work with analytical constructs based on variables such as speaker, hearer, setting, topic, and channel, for example. A corollary to the phenomenon of variation is the occurrence of styles of speaking, or registers. As one sociolinguist has stated, 'There are no single-style speakers' (Labov 1970). Every speaker adopts a style of speaking which is appropriate to the particular social context.

The research focus of sociolinguistics has ranged from topics external to the code of language itself, for example the area of language planning and policy-making (see chapter 1), through studies of language linked to social variables, for example men's and women's language and terms of address, to the study of norms for interacting, for example studies of telephone talk and teacher talk. A key concept in sociolinguistics is focus on the speech community rather than on an individual or idealized speaker as the focus of language.

Of consequence to the language teaching profession is the fact that sociolinguistics deals explicitly with languages in ways that have far-reaching significance for their teaching and learning, particularly the question: *What* language do we teach? In terms of our discussion, sociolinguistics plays a vital role in influencing the specification of language content in a communicative syllabus.

Of the various thrusts of sociolinguistics during the past twenty years, probably the concept of communicative competence has had the greatest impact on the field of language pedagogy. Since Hymes' 1972 paper on the topic, the concept of communicative competence has continued to develop. Though not all would define it in exactly the same way, a generally accepted definition begins with the idea that communicative competence entails knowing not only the language code or the form of language, but also what to say to whom and how to say it appropriately in any given situation. It deals with the social and cultural knowledge that speakers are presumed to have which enables them to use and interpret linguistic forms. It also includes knowledge of who may speak or may not speak in certain settings, when to speak and when to remain silent, how to talk to persons of different statuses and roles. A well-known description of communicative competence has been that it includes knowledge of what to say, when, how, where, and to whom. In effect, it takes in all of the verbal and non-verbal mechanisms which native speakers use unconsciously to communicate with each other.

4.2   A cognitively-based view of language learning

Course planning which centers around learners and their needs must concern itself with individual differences in learning styles. Awareness of the need to attend to such differences is not new, but recently second language research has looked at individual traits much more seriously. Moreover, the growing emphasis on cognitive psychology and information processing models in education in general has given special impetus to the area of research related to language learning (Rivers and Melvin,

1981). For curriculum planning and material development, the emphasis is to design tasks that will allow learners to experience a variety of cognitive activities. Thus, ideally, both teachers and students will become aware of individual learning styles.

4.2.1 Strategies and tactics

Second language researchers have long been plagued by the fact that language learners exhibit both high levels of systematicity and considerable variance in their acquisition processes. One question arising from this state of affairs is the need to distinguish between universal learning processes that might be common to all language learners as opposed to idiosyncratic features that are specific to individuals. McLaughlin (1981) distinguishes between 'acquisition heuristics' which are the universal processes, probably consisting of language-specific as well as general cognitive mechanisms that are utilized by all learners while learning language, and individual 'operating procedures' which are idiosyncratic features.

A more operational distinction for our purposes is the one made by Seliger (1983) between strategies and tactics. Strategies, according to Seliger, are superordinate, abstract, constant, and long-term cognitive processes. These are general cognitive mechanisms employed by all learners regardless of language background, age, or acquisitional context. Thus, for instance, all learners will employ such cognitive processes as hypothesis testing, simplification, and overgeneralization. On the other hand, individual learners develop their unique, specially-suited tactics to cope with learning tasks. Tactics are therefore short-term processes used to overcome temporary and immediate obstacles to the achievement of the long-range goal of language acquisition. Such tactics take the form of rule using, memorization, mnemonic devices, input utilization techniques and the like. Learners may not have any control over strategies which are innate in nature, but they could probably be made aware of their own tactics as well as those used by others and be shown which tactics work better for them.

Since Rubin (1975) drew second language researchers' attention to the characteristics of the 'good language learner', we have not stopped our quest for a better description of these characteristics, assuming that if we knew what the good language learner does naturally, we could help all other learners attempt to employ the same techniques. Research relevant to material development has been carried out by Cohen and Hosenfeld (1981) in the area of mentalistic techniques utilized by language learners and reported by them via introspection. These kinds of studies tap the tactics of which language learners are aware or can be made aware.

4.2.2   Context-embedded and context-reduced language use

One of the perplexing characteristics of second language acquisition is the difference that seems to exist between the strategies or processes needed for acquiring the language in its natural environment (outside school) and learning it as a school subject (in the classroom). Educators cannot fail to observe that immigrant children from literate, middle-class backgrounds who have been exposed to more abstract vocabulary, or have been sensitized to both context-reduced and decontextualized use of language in their first language can cope with the task of second language learning in the school environment more readily than children from lower-class backgrounds who have little experience with decontextualized language even in their first language. One explanation for this difference is offered by Cummins (1978, 1979, 1980) in his 'interdependence hypothesis'. According to Cummins, the cognitive-academic aspects of a first and second language are thought to be interdependent, and proficiency in a second language in a school setting is predicted to depend largely on previous learning of literacy-related functions of language. Cummins calls these functions CALP (cognitive, academic language proficiency) and they require a context reduced use of language. CALP can be empirically distinguished from BICS (basic interpersonal communicative skills) which are more relevant to the natural settings where interpersonal communication takes place.

Cummins (1981) argues for a continuum of contextual support available for expressing and receiving meaning. At one end of the continuum we find context-embedded communication where meaning is actively negotiated by the participants, while at the other end there is context-reduced communication. In context-embedded communication the participants can rely on various non-linguistic elements which help support meaning when the linguistic features are not sufficient. In a context-reduced situation, the participants need to rely much more extensively on linguistic clues. Cummins' context continuum is intersected by another continuum based on the amount of information processing that is involved in the task; tasks that are well-learned and automated require little cognitive effort, while those that are not well-learned require more cognitive involvement. Thus the most difficult situation is one which is context-reduced with a cognitively demanding task. The relevance of Cummins' explanation to language learning is that we need to distinguish between language used in everyday, face-to-face interaction where fluency or communication strategies may be of greatest importance and school settings where the learning tasks are much more cognitively demanding.

In terms of application to EFL/ESL course and materials development, Cummins' ideas lead to a number of important principles:

1. In defining course objectives, we must first consider the learners' proficiency and general development in their L1 at course entry; accordingly, expectations with respect to fluency in the target language and expectations concerning academic skills in the new language can be suited to the particular student population.
2. In developing learning tasks, careful attention needs to be given to the level of cognitive ability which is required for the fulfillment of the tasks. Tasks, therefore, should be presented in a graded sequence from those that are less to more demanding. (See 5.2.3.)
3. In designing activities for language use, learners should be guided from context-embedded to context-reduced situations, enabling them to develop the necessary skills to interact in the latter.
4. In planning the overall course, we need to incorporate both fluency-oriented work leading towards face-to-face communication and accuracy work leading to better cognitive and academic language proficiency. The incorporation of both aspects of language acquisition will enable learners to develop both their interpersonal communicative strategies and the academic language skills needed for successful scholastic work.

4.2.3   The holistic approach to language learning

Learning theory was greatly influenced by behavioristic psychology in the 1950s and 1960s. As a result, course objectives were apt to be defined in behavioristic or performance terms: 'What will the students' behavior be like at the end of the course?' In order to achieve such terminal behavior goals, students had to be put through a carefully sequenced and rather intensive practice period. At each point in the progression, 'positive' behavior was reinforced while 'negative' behavior was rejected. Thus, repeating a dialogue presented in a textbook from memory could be viewed as positive behavior while expressing one's own thoughts in inaccurate English was usually discouraged. Such an approach led, of course, to emphasis on linguistic form at the expense of meaning and communication. As a result, too, many learners were capable of producing perfect sentences in practice sessions but this ability would typically break down when they were faced with situations in which real communication was necessary.

Furthermore, focus on accuracy demanded concentration on discrete points in the language. Such discrete points were the basis for both activities in the learning process and for testing achievement. Perhaps the most misleading notion resulting from the behavioristic influence in language learning was the assumption that a succession of similar activities (pattern practice) devoted to separate structural features would eventually lead to communicative competence.

Critics of the behavioral approach to learning maintained that such a view of the learning process curbs creativity and self-expression, ignores cognitive processes, and overlooks personality traits of the specific learners; a holistic approach to learning, on the other hand, would incorporate all three of these aspects (Titone 1981). As a result of criticism of behaviorism, learning theorists have tended to return to the earlier Gestalt psychology, transforming it into cognitive-field theory and discovery learning. In these approaches, perception, motivation, and theoretical deductivity become strongly emphasized. Particularly important in this work has been the influence of Maslow's (1954) humanistic psychology (also known as holistic-dynamic) which suggests a much more comprehensive perspective of motivation than that of the behaviorist response-reinforcement theory.

In the recent era, language learning theory has been reshaped to incorporate a mentalistic-cognitivist view which is compatible with a holistic approach to learning in general. At the same time, language learning theory has also shifted its emphasis from linguistic competence to sociocultural appropriateness and communicative competence, influenced by developments in sociolinguistics.

During the behavioristic period when considerable attention was given to concentration on separate elements of linguistic form as a basis for activities, learning situations, and testing items, the materials developed were divided into units centered around a specific linguistic element, for example, a tense, an inflectional form, or some other linguistic point. A communicative orientation to learning and teaching, on the other hand, places high value on overall interaction and on message transmission, so by definition it is not compatible with a discrete point view of language learning. It is the integrative (holistic) view, emphasizing the totality of language learning, which works best with a communicative approach. It becomes obvious, therefore, that the development that led towards a shift from accuracy and form to appropriateness and meaning has also led from a discrete view to a holistic perspective.

4.2.4   What learners' errors tell us

Another important shift in current thinking about language learning theory is the attitude towards learners' errors. If in the 1960s errors had to be avoided at all costs, today errors are viewed as an integral part of the language-learning process from which we can gain very significant insights. The question of universality becomes relevant again, the issues being: (a) To what extent do errors made by second language learners represent transfers from the first language system? (b) To what extent do they exhibit universal characteristics of developmental features (since they often resemble errors made by first-language learners)?

Researchers have often suggested the hypothesis-testing process as the most important explanation of second language learning. Schachter (1981) shows how learners of a target language when faced with a problem in the new language will infer from previous knowledge (their L1) and from their newly gained experience in L2. Accordingly, they will try to identify the domain within which the problem occurs (an example of domain is 'main verb') and then look for a solution within that domain by making a hypothesis about it. The potential errors that might result can be due to the wrong choice of the domain, the wrong choice of a hypothesis, or a combination of both. This explains why learners from the same language background may come up with different errors, and why conversely speakers of different language backgrounds can make similar errors, both by employing this hypothesis-testing process. Furthermore, as the learners' experience in the target language expands, domains and hypotheses are chosen according to newly acquired experiences and these might reflect developmental errors more profusely. Materials developers need to be aware of such hypothesis-testing processes in designing learning tasks.

4.3   The fundamentals of a humanistic curriculum

In many instances, communicative language programs have incorporated educational philosophies based on humanistic psychology, or a view which in the context of goals for other subject areas has been called 'the humanistic curriculum' (McNeil 1977). Indeed, the postulates it advocates are familiar to all who enjoyed the period of 'greening' (Reich 1970) in North American life in the late 1960s and early 1970s. In broader educational terms, such a curriculum fosters sharing of control, negotiation, and joint responsibility by co-participants; it stresses thinking, feelings, and action; it attempts to relate subject matter to learners' basic needs and lives; and it advances the self as a legitimate object of learning. The deepest goal or purpose is to develop the whole person within a human society (McNeil 1977).

Based on views which are drawn from the school of humanistic psychology – notably represented by Abraham Maslow, Carl Rogers, Fritz Perls, and Erich Berne – this tradition exerted an important influence on the field of education in the United States resulting in learner-centered pedagogy and confluent educational practices which combine affective and cognitive objectives. In concrete terms, the humanistic curriculum puts high value on people accepting responsibility for their own learning, making decisions for themselves, choosing and initiating activities, expressing feelings and opinions about needs, abilities, and preferences. In this framework, the teacher acts as a facilitator of others' learning rather than as an implanter of knowledge. Cooperation between learners and teachers is stressed.

Within the international community of language pedagogy, the humanistic view was reflected in the important shift which took place in the early 1970s when learners' needs for acquiring new languages became the central issue in general methodology as reflected in the work done within the Council of Europe and in some of the new theoretical developments in Britain. In fact, emphasis on learner-centered pedagogy has probably also helped to bring about the expanded view of product/outcomes as indicated by the language for special purposes movement, and in the detailed checklists found in Munby's work (1978) which result in needs profiles of single learners. Attitudes about the humanistic tone and intent of a language classroom are often implicit in writings on communicative goals in language teaching; however, some authors make them quite explicit. For example, Morrow (1981:63) states: 'Learning becomes to a large extent the learner's responsibility.'

In operational terms, a language program which draws on humanistic curriculum goals tries to achieve these objectives:

1. Great emphasis is placed on meaningful communication from the learner's point of view; texts should be authentic, tasks should be communicative, outcomes should be negotiated and not predetermined.
2. The learner is the focal point of this approach and respect for the individual is highly valued.
3. Learning is viewed as a self-realization experience in which the learner has considerable say in the decision-making process.
4. Other learners are viewed as a support group within which they interact, help, and evaluate themselves and each other, as well as the whole process.
5. The teacher is a facilitator who is more concerned with class atmosphere than with the adherence to the syllabus or the materials in use. The latter should serve the students' needs.
6. The first language of the learner is viewed as a useful aid when it is necessary for understanding and for formulating hypotheses about the target language, particularly in the early stages.

4.4   Exploring the roles of teachers, learners and others within a communicative curriculum

The infusion of humanistic values in courses with communicative goals has been indicated most strikingly through discussions of roles for teachers and learners (Fanselow 1977, Allwright 1972). In fact, the metaphor of the cooperative enterprise which is advocated for communicative language teaching has been characterized as one of teach/learn (Pit Corder 1977). In this role-relationship between teachers and learners, their endeavors take place in a cooperative, open, and caring manner. The teacher is there to guide learners, not to tell them. The teacher's role is recognized as a facilitating one, with learners proceeding according to their own inner capacities, not in a lock-step plan solely of the teacher's creation. An attitude of cooperation and sharing is stressed, as well as an emphasis on group activities.

A central theme is that it is the teacher's responsibility to lessen any feelings learners may have of anxiety or fear. Learners should not feel shy about speaking or asking questions. At no time should they try to avoid having the teacher call on them because of feeling timid or insecure. 'Keeping a low profile' in order not to be called on by the teacher is not in keeping with the atmosphere in a language classroom where communicative objectives are stressed (Littlewood 1981:93).

4.4.1 *Teaching/learning as a metaphor*

Course designers and material writers by offering methodological guidelines can also build in assumptions about the role relationships between teacher and learners in the instructional plans which they create. Viewed this way, teaching/learning is a metaphor which embodies a catalog of values and attitudes about the social behavior which should take place in classrooms. Thus teaching/learning as a figure of speech can sum up many of the features regarding humanistically-oriented educational goals.

Metaphors are convenient because after they have become established writers no longer have to spell out long rationales or present elaborate guidelines; instead, they need only evoke the metaphor and we all understand the intended meaning. In such a way the metaphor of teaching/learning has come to embody the cooperative spirit and intent of a humanistic classroom.

Probably for most of the world the role-relationship in classrooms which is most widely embraced and understood as a metaphor is that of pedagogue/pupil, or the teacher as a person who puts knowledge into the head of the student. It is a metaphor which has been part of western civilization since the time of Plato, at least. In it the pedagogue is the source of information; pupils seek wisdom. But in dealing with communicative goals, pedagogue/pupil is insufficient on many counts, not the least of which is that in a communicative classroom learners do not remain seated at the feet of the master. Rather, they frequently move about in order to interact with each other.

4.4.2   Is teaching/learning adequate?

As a way of capturing the essentials of communicative language teaching, is the metaphor teaching/learning adequate? The work which must be accomplished in a program which has adopted communicative objectives is in a different mode than other subject areas in the school curriculum. True enough, the language class, like other classes, is a social encounter. But therein lies the paradox: in a language class where the objective is language use, the material to 'learn' so to speak, can only be 'mastered' by the learners engaging in a social encounter, or by experiencing the social behavior of and their personal role in the target culture – almost a play within a play. The language classroom becomes a place to rehearse, try-out, and try-on new cultural roles and identities, or at least extensions of old ones. Although teaching/learning does not interfere with these objectives, it does nothing which dynamically contributes to meeting them.

In fact, the roles of teaching/learning as articulated by ESL/EFL specialists have not been expanded, altered or modified beyond what they would be for any other subject matter in a general, humanistically-oriented curriculum. The interesting examples are CLL (Community Language Learning) and Suggestopedia: both were initially developed and used for any and all subjects – not necessarily language instruction.

When the emphasis is on doing, particularly in group activities, more than on knowing or caring, then the role of teacher takes on a different configuration from that of a facilitator. The focus is not on one-to-one relationships necessarily, but more on getting other people to do things – with language. This does not mean in any way that teachers in communicatively-oriented classrooms need to abandon their own personal values regarding humanistic learning and teaching. But everyone in the language learning enterprise – teachers, learners and the rest who contribute to it – need more adequate metaphors to work with in order to carry out communicative objectives.

4.4.3   Cross-cultural implications

To a certain extent, the teach part of the relationship is embodied unconsciously by a generation of native-speaker ESL/EFL instructors who embrace humanistic values in education, bringing them into their teaching practically without thinking about it as part of their cultural baggage, so to speak. The role of the facilitating teacher, a person who is an empathetic listener, capable of and even expecting to have one-to-one classroom relationships with learners, is another characteristic that is widely worn by many native-speaker teachers, like a familiar garment.

However, the fact that the role of facilitator often does not fit non-native teachers whose own backgrounds did not include exposure to the same kinds of educational values is sometimes overlooked by ELT specialists who plan courses and write materials for the EFL marketplace. Unconsciously, they may even regard this as a problematic area, a place where 'they' will have to change to fit 'our' ways. The result, at best, is a cross-cultural stand-off. Unfortunately, what is at risk is the opportunity for an EFL program which might otherwise benefit from it to actively carry out communicative goals because the tone and intent of the materials did not match the teachers' perceptions of accepted roles for themselves and learners.

We are reminded, too, that most English language teachers in the world are non-native; in fact, they tend to have a less than fluent command of the language they teach. On the other hand, they have the very significant advantage of knowing the learners' first language and most likely coming themselves from the learners' cultural background. Furthermore, they are thoroughly familiar with the educational system within which they teach; in fact, they are usually the products of the same system. Since the English teacher in the non-native environment must continually observe local conditions, adopting ways which are appropriate to the region's standards for the teaching profession (Strevens 1980), the non-native teacher might be better suited for the job. However, the humanistic curriculum as such might develop a variety of local versions, each one suited to the particular area and conditions where English is taught for communicative purposes.

Another facet of the cultural mismatch inherent in teaching/learning roles entails the learner's role. Much has been written about the spirit of education which takes place in humanistically-oriented classrooms. As their part in the social relationship, the communicative approach assumes learners will take responsibility for their own learning, and help formulate goals for courses through processes of negotiation (Littlewood 1981). It is assumed that such endeavors take place in a spirit of cooperation, since learners must be primarily concerned with the goal of learning, not of grades, meeting requirements, or fulfilling societal obligations of countless kinds.

Even the staunchest advocates of teaching/learning realize that this characterization, though broadly drawn, holds out an unrealistic picture of real learners at all ages in most circumstances – ESL and EFL. What course designers should consider is that to achieve teaching/learning many intermediate steps need to be provided that will act to imbue participants in a communicatively-oriented course with an understanding of its underlying values. In effect, attitudes and expectations must change. Instead of expecting the teacher to make all the decisions, learners need to develop initiative and willingness to take on part of the responsibilities. This can take place while the participants are engaged in carrying out tasks linked to language learning, but it means that part of the course design will be overtly directed to establishing new role identities that are more closely related to the purpose of communicative language use and which might be significantly different from the roles to which learners had been hitherto accustomed.

4.4.4   Developing alternative metaphors

Nattinger (1984) suggests that 'communicative language teaching has become a new metaphor in ESL/EFL language acquisition.' Similarly, still within the fold of humanistically-oriented educational goals, our purpose is to build alternative metaphors for describing the roles of teachers and learners that can be used effectively by material writers and course designers. In order to take full advantage of the communicative teaching metaphor, planners must build on new role definitions for learners and teachers as well. Teachers can no longer be viewed as having absolute authority to plan lessons, choose learning content, decide on all the activities and be fully in control of everything that goes on during the learning process. Even the term 'facilitator' cannot suffice since it has been used for over a decade and is therefore identified with various methodological concepts which may not be useful for the purpose. New metaphors are needed which will encompass the new roles teachers fulfill in the communicative classroom. Similarly, learners cannot continue to be viewed as passive receivers of information. They need to make decisions and choices which transmit some of the planning of the process to them. Just to say that learners will take on more responsibility will not do.

Within the classroom setting, there are many facets upon which to capitalize while searching for new metaphors. For one, the classroom context serves as a microcosm, a world in miniature, of the real world outside, but it can never be exactly the same. It has a dimension of its own that demands special consideration. In the classroom, the teacher is involved with staging, creating an atmosphere, and moving participants in space. For learners, a communicative language classroom has the potential to be a stage for trying out a new culture-language identity or extending one's present identity by adding a new language dimension. An alternative metaphor should be one which writers can easily use in their scripts and scenarios to give directions to participants, personify their roles, and set the tone for activities. By building roles into the instructional materials which symbolize communicative goals, more can be accomplished towards bringing them about than through any other way.

TEACHER AS DIRECTOR

The director's role in a communicative classroom is essentially a creative one in which the prime function is getting other people to do things with language by establishing short-term objectives which coincide with the interests of the majority in the group. Just as the theater director plays a pivotal role in sustaining the fiction of a stage drama, so the teacher/director uses the classroom stage to simulate the real world. But because it is a special world, the director imbues it with a bit of excitement, at times even mystery.

On a human level, the director makes personal connections between the scenario and each of the players, helping each one to understand the script, and interpreting parts that are unclear. The director, too, provides strong psychological support by being an individual and a group morale booster. The director has the ability to project an attitude of being interested in each individual player's performance, allowing enough freedom of choice so that ultimately each individual's personal style is reflected in his/her performance.

The director provides overall coherence by focusing on goals that are long-range, at the same time carefully explaining short-term objectives. Outside of class, the director connects with professional peers by sharing ideas and exchanging visits to each other's productions. On the practical side, the director attends to time-keeping, getting everybody in and out on-time, manages assignments and coordinates the use of hands-on materials. Along with this, the director attends to all the necessary props, supports, and realia which must be available to make the proceedings work smoothly.

LEARNERS AS PLAYERS

The terms *play* and *players* hold out a rich potential for developing a metaphor concerning language learners. Only superficially is play a recreational activity, confined to the interests of children. Psychologists, ethnologists and anthropologists point out how play is practice for all of the more serious endeavors of the species (Bruner 1972). In fact, even sub-human primates use highly ritualized body and facial movements to signify to each other that a particular behavior is not to be taken seriously, or 'is for play' as contrasted with behavior that entails the rights and responsibilities of real-life (Bateson 1955). In many ways, the characteristics of play suggest fruitful possibilities for incorporating into course designs in terms of the developmental, maturational, and social growth of learners.

As a player, one must participate actively. At the same time, one must concentrate by observing what others do. Players take part in all of the interactional configurations which are important in a communicative language course: as individuals, in pairs, in small groups, and in whole group displays. As players, participants can come to view language learning as something quite different from 'knowing' which they associate with other schooling experiences in their lives.

Another facet of playing is found in the theory of games and gaming. Games, of course, are carried out by players. Because of their inherent structure, games aptly lend themselves to language-learning workouts. But the scope of games goes far beyond the popular use of the term. Players in a game are required to focus on objectives, follow clearly stated rules, and perform tasks both cooperatively and competitively. Games, too, contain an element of suspension of belief in the present – or losing oneself in the activity – that makes for a successful language-learning experience.

Particularly for adults, play has a vitally serious dimension which needs to be captured in the materials. Adult players expect to be challenged; they are not satisfied with unnecessary, repetitive procedures. Adult players are more apt to connect the new language content to their own real-life needs since they direct their attention more to meaningful objectives than to the details of blackboard exercises. Moreover, adult players will reject topics or themes in materials which demean their own backgrounds.

The adult learner will never be a child again, but he will not be without 'the heritage of those former states' (Erikson 1972:702). In writing about play, Erikson compares a child's solitary play with the construction of 'the function of a dramatic performance in adulthood'. But Erikson then goes on to wonder 'which is metaphorical for what?' He points out that the adult, when involved with the play of theater, manages to get engaged with 'a certain abandon, with intensified loyalty, and often with increased energy and efficiency.' One must be amazed by how close Erikson came to describing the quality which a good language program must possess if communicative goals are to be realized by the players.

ROLES FOR OTHERS: PRODUCERS, WRITERS, AND TREND-SETTERS

Ways are needed by which to bring into focus others' roles beyond those performed by teachers and learners. These others are usually responsible for making decisions that pertain to larger numbers than just the people in one classroom. Furthermore, their influence is often pervasive:

1.   *Administrators as producers*

In an academic context, the entrepreneurial role of program administrators is often obscured. Yet there are parallels between the position and that carried out by producers in the theatrical world. Administrators as producers are concerned with finances, making projections about future growth, and looking for new audiences. Language program producers are also involved with others in answering the vital *what* question concerning course content. In addition, they set plans for instruction over levels, years, forms, or grades, acting as intermediaries between performances in the classroom and the concerns of those who have a vital interest in what takes place there: parents, inspectors, ministry representatives, etc.

2. Writers

In a communicative framework, writers must produce materials that encourage and lead to spontaneous behavior in classrooms. Writers represent the profession's best possibility to move on from what one classroom researcher (Allwright 1982) has described as the cycle of presentation, testing, and feedback which constitutes much of the activity in typical classrooms. In order to carry out this difficult assignment, writers of communicative course materials need both general and specific expertise. In terms of their general background, writers must have up-to-date understanding of linguistic and learning theories, broad knowledge of the cultural patterns pertaining to the target language as well as to the learners' first language, and familiarity with the educational context within which their materials will be utilized.

The more specific expertise of writers relates to the actual form in which the materials are to be realized. In fact, writers are primarily concerned with providing language input since they produce the scripts and scenarios for use by directors and players. Writers need to have a well-developed sense of the complexity of scripts, their internal workings, and their types. For example, they should know that scripts can run the gamut from being restricted to open-ended. Similarly, they can be on a scale from controlled to self-determined. By recognizing writing as a serious craft, as a worthwhile role to play, more professionalism may emerge in this area. At present, there is a great need for developing standards, evaluation criteria, and general expertise in the writing of materials for language programs.

3. L2 Researchers as trend-setters

It is not to the point here to retrace discussions regarding the relationship between research and language pedagogy. Rather, since the effect of academic activity in the language teaching field is pervasive, it is only necessary to ask: In terms of the metaphor that has been developed, where do academic types fit in? Certainly, researchers establish the basis for a curriculum by their influence in the fields of language science, learning theory and educational philosophy. When looked at over a period of time, this influence could be viewed as one of changing fashions, or of changing outlooks (Kelly 1969). It might be most appropriate, therefore, to characterize the role of researchers as that of trend-setters, or people who by the internal demands of their own professions – producing scholarly writings and exchanges – set styles. The term 'researchers', of course, takes in both those who are concerned with evidence derived from experimental work as well as those 'thinkers' whose commentaries provide us with deeper understandings of theoretical constructs.

Is their influence direct or indirect? In the case of the scholar who first developed the concept of communicative competence, Del Hymes, the effort had nothing to do with second language teaching, having been originally addressed to ethnographers as a programmatic statement about what the workers in that field should be attending to (Hymes 1962). Moreover, it has been pointed out that among current L2 researchers each tends to work in a unique, personal style (Schumann 1982). This insight prepares us to regard the product of hypothesis-making more in terms of artful displays than as sources of concrete information. But a community needs the zest and imagination of creative personalities. In this sense, L2 researchers as cultural fashion-setters make a vital contribution to the language-teaching profession.

Practical applications

1. Discuss the relevance of the following with respect to an EFL or an ESL context with which you are familiar:
   a) the sociocultural view of language
   b) the holistic approach to learning
   c) the humanistic curriculum
2. Examine the texts for two courses, one reflecting an audiolingual approach, the other reflecting a communicative approach to language learning. How do the two books differ with respect to:
   a) sociocultural views on the nature of language?
   b) cognitive views on the nature of language learning?
   c) humanistic views of education?
3. Develop a language learning task in which you try to incorporate the major principles of the communicative approach. Try out the task with your peers and then lead a feedback session in which the task is evaluated. Write down your thoughts about the task:
   a) before trying it out with the others
   b) after trying it out
   c) immediately after the feedback session
   Is it possible to observe a gradual process which leads to the improvement of the task? If so, can you describe the process?
4. Organize a debate or panel discussion around the issues presented in section 4.4. The participants express their views, either pro or

con, on the effectiveness of teaching/learning as a metaphor in various settings, for example ESL and EFL. The panel members should feel free to comment on other instructional styles as well: for example, authoritarian, permissive, Socratic, etc.

References

Allwright, R. L. 1972. 'Prescription and description in the training of language teachers'. In J. Qvistgaard, H. Schwarts, and H. Spang-Hanssen (Eds.) *Proceedings of the third International Congress of Applied Linguistics* (AILA: Copenhagen, 1972), pp. 150–66. Heidelberg: Julius Groos Verlag.

Allwright, R. L. 1982. Talk before faculty and students, Master's program in Applied Linguistics, University of So. California (March).

Bateson, G. 1955. 'A theory of play and fantasy'. In J. S. Bruner, A. Jolly and K. Sylva (Eds.) *Play, its role in development and evolution*, pp. 119–29. 1976. Harmondsworth: Penguin Books.

Bruner, J. S. 1972. 'Nature and uses of immaturity'. In J. S. Bruner, A. Jolly and K. Sylva (Eds.) *Play, its role in development and evolution*, pp. 28–64. 1976. Harmondsworth: Penguin Books.

Cohen, A. D. and C. Hosenfeld. 1981. 'Some mentalistic data in second language research'. *Language Learning* 31(2), pp. 285–313.

Corder, S. Pit. 1977. 'Language teaching and learning: a social encounter'. In H. Brown, C. Yorio, and R. Crymes (Eds.) *On TESOL '77. Teaching and learning English as a second language: trends in research and practice*. Washington, D.C. TESOL.

Cummins, J. 1978. 'Bilingualism and the development of metalinguistic awareness'. *Journal of Cross-Cultural Psychology* 9, pp. 131–49.

Cummins, J. 1979. 'Cognitive/academic language proficiency, linguistic interdependence, the optimal age question and some other matters'. *Working Papers in Bilingualism* 19, pp. 197–205.

Cummins, J. 1980. 'The construct of language proficiency in bilingual education'. Paper presented at the Georgetown Round Table on Languages and Linguistics.

Cummins, J. 1981. *The role of primary language development in promoting educational success for language minority students. Schooling and language minority students: A theoretical framework*. Los Angeles: Evaluation, Dissemination, and Assessment Center, California State University, Los Angeles.

Erikson, E. H. 1972. 'Play and actuality'. In J. S. Bruner, A. Jolly and K. Sylva (Eds.) *Play, its role in development and evolution*, pp. 688–703. 1976. Harmondsworth: Penguin Books.

Fanselow, J. F. 1977. 'Beyond Rashomon – conceptualizing and describing the teaching act'. *TESOL Quarterly* 11(1), pp. 17–39.

Hymes, D. H. 1962. 'The ethnography of speaking'. In T. Gladwin and W. Sturtevant (Eds.) *Anthropology and human behavior*, pp. 13–53. Washington, D.C.: Anthropological Society of Washington.

Hymes, D. H. 1972. 'On communicative competence'. In J. B. Pride and J. Holmes (Eds.) *Sociolinguistics*. Harmondsworth: Penguin Books.

Kelly, L. G. 1969. *25 centuries of language teaching*. Rowley, Massachusetts: Newbury House.

Labov, W. 1970. 'The study of language in its social context'. *Studium Generale*. 23, pp. 30–87.

Littlewood, W. 1981. *Communicative language teaching*. Cambridge: Cambridge University Press.

Maslow, A. 1954. *Motivation and personality*. New York: Harper.

McLaughlin, B. 1981. 'Difference and similarities between first and second language learning'. In Winitz (Ed.) *Native language and foreign language acquisition*. New York: Annals of the New York Academy of Sciences, vol. 379.

McNeil, J. D. 1977. *Curriculum: a comprehensive introduction*. Boston, Massachusetts: Little, Brown and Company.

Morrow, K. 1981. 'Principles of communicative methodology'. In K. Johnson and K. Morrow (Eds.) *Communication in the classroom*. Harlow: Longman.

Munby, J. 1978. *Communicative syllabus design*. Cambridge: Cambridge University Press.

Nattinger, J. R. 1984. 'Communicative language teaching: a new metaphor'. *TESOL Quarterly* 18 (3), pp. 391–407.

Reich, C. A. 1970. *The greening of America*. New York: Random House.

Rivers, W. and B. J. Melvin. 1981. 'Language learners as individuals: discovering their needs, wants and learning styles'. In Alatis, Altman and Alatis (Eds.) *The second language classroom: directions for the 1980s*, pp. 79–93. New York: Oxford University Press.

Rubin, J. 1975. 'What the good language learner can teach us'. *TESOL Quarterly* 9, pp. 41–51.

Schachter, J. 1981. 'A new account of language transfer'. Paper presented at Language Transfer Conference, Ann Arbor, Michigan.

Schumann, J. H. 1982. 'Art and science in second language acquisition research'. In M. Clark and J. Handscombe (Eds.) *On TESOL '82. Pacific perspectives on language learning and teaching*, pp. 107–24. Washington DC: TESOL.

Seliger, H. W. 1983. 'Strategy and tactic in second language acquisition'. In K. M. Bailey (Ed.) *Proceedings of the third Los Angeles second language research forum*. Rowley, Massachusetts: Newbury House.

Strevens, P. 1980. *Teaching English as an international language: from practice to principle*. Oxford: Pergamon Press.

Titone, R. 1981. 'The holistic approach to second language education'. In Alatis, Altman, and Alatis (Eds.) *The second language classroom: directions for the 1980s*, pp. 67–77. New York: Oxford University Press.

Other suggested readings

Chomsky, N. 1965. *Aspects of the theory of syntax*. Cambridge, Massachusetts: M.I.T. Press.

Gumperz, J. J. 1970. 'Verbal strategies in multilingual communication'. In
  J. E. Alatis (Ed.) *21st Annual Georgetown Round Table on Languages and
  Linguistics*, pp. 129–47.

5 The scope of a communicative syllabus

Overview

Communicative goals have produced profound changes in the three dimensions of a syllabus. In language content, the shift has been marked by an enlargement in the scope of the entire area. The process zone has been emphasized through attention to global, cognitive, and creative practices which we will call 'workouts'. The product area has reflected re-emphasized interest in the language skills, particularly reading and writing. Although the communicative approach may not always create radical changes, it has affected our view of the way in which course outcomes are presented, defined, and evaluated.

There are, however, prevailing misconceptions regarding the communicative approach to language learning. One such frequently expressed misunderstanding is the belief held by many that it is a new methodology which has come to replace the structural approach. The intention of this chapter is to show that the communicative approach is not a system which replaces older ones, but rather alters and expands the components of the existing ones in terms of language content, course products, and learning processes. The most significant contribution of the communicative approach is that it has brought about a more comprehensive view of language teaching and learning.

As indicated in diagram 6, the communicative syllabus has expanded in all of the three areas which comprise the components of a syllabus.

5.1 Expansion of the language content dimension

Communicative goals have brought about a more comprehensive view of the language component. Consequently, content in the curriculum has been expanded to include not only structures, situations, and themes or topics, but also concepts (notions) and functions.

5.1.1 Conceptual and functional meaning

The content of an utterance can be considered in terms of two major types of meaning: (a) the propositional or conceptual meaning of an

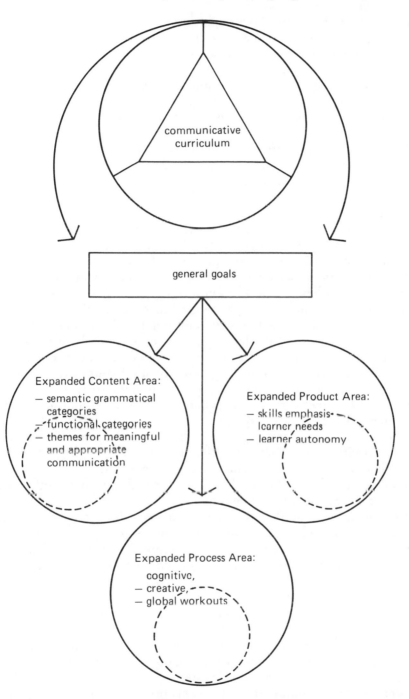

Diagram 6   An altered map of language content, process, and product

utterance, and (b) its illocutionary force. The conceptual meaning expresses our perception of events, entities, states, causes, location, time, etc., including grammatical elements such as agents and instruments. In a syllabus, these elements are realized as notions or semantico-grammatical categories. On the other hand, the illocutionary force of an utterance expresses its functional meaning: whether the particular utterance functions in a certain context as a request, an apology, an invitation, etc.

Thus, a person late for a meeting might walk in and say: 'There was a terrible traffic jam on Wilshire Blvd.' The conceptual meaning is simply a description of the state of traffic on the street, but its illocutionary force is to function as an apology for being late to the meeting. Similarly, an expression such as 'it's hot in here' can communicate both conceptual meaning about the temperature in the room and illocutionary force which functions as a request for opening the door or window.

According to Wilkins (1976), the notional syllabus which he proposed can incorporate conceptual and functional components into a learning/teaching syllabus. The key questions that need to be answered in course designing are no longer related to specific units or structural points, as was the case with a structural syllabus. Now, questions relate to the overall goals of the language course. Such goals, when defined in general terms, advocate 'language use for communicative purposes'. Thus, Wilkins says: 'In drawing up a notional syllabus instead of asking how speakers of the language express themselves, or when and where they use the language, we ask what it is they communicate through language.' The key questions are:

1. What kind of semantico-grammatical knowledge does a learner need to have in order to communicative effectively?
2. What kind of skills are needed for communication?
3. What types of learning/teaching activities will contribute to the acquisition of the communicative skills?

In a notional syllabus, the focus on grammar is no longer just the internalization of rules, but rather a view of grammar within a communicative framework. In other words, once the communicative task is defined we can select structural features necessary to complete it.

Wilkins (1976) advocates a notional organization of the syllabus because he sees considerable pedagogic advantages in approaching a notion such as temporal relations logically. Since the ability to express time concepts is an important aspect of our communicative potential, it is important to provide the learner with the various linguistic means that might be used to express the most important time relations.

The focus on notions, as suggested by Wilkins, presents syllabus designers with a number of very serious problems. First, as mentioned by Brumfit (1981) in reaction to Wilkins (1981), focus on notions seems to entail the idea that notions are clearly definable and that the relations holding between them can be fully specified. This, however, is not yet the case. Perhaps the best way to illustrate the difficulty involved is by looking at the plan of specification in *Roget's Thesaurus*. The categories and their sub-categories seem to be logically very appealing. One marvels at the intricate organization of the various semantic concepts and at the level of cross-reference embedded in it. The detailed plan of classification given at the beginning of the book is a valuable contribution to aid our understanding of how the Thesaurus works.

However, as users of the Thesaurus we may never even glance at the synopsis of categories because the classes in it are counter-intuitive to the way in which we organize our thoughts about the world around us. It seems to make more sense for the lay person to relate to actual language events in the real world than to semantic notions. Thus, for instance, in writing, one may look up some familiar concept in the Thesaurus in order to expand one's understanding of that concept or avail oneself of various lexical choices which the language provides. But it is very unlikely that one will start out by using the synopsis of categories. Instead, one turns to the alphabetical and numerical cross-reference system, never looking at the semantic specifications.

As is the case with using the Thesaurus, using a notional inventory for the planning of a global course syllabus may be helpful in relating the content to communicative needs of the learners, yet this may not translate easily into teaching/learning units. Wilkins (1981) recognizes this problem. First he mentions the fact that there is to date no systematic notional grammar in existence which could serve as a basis for our decision-making process. Secondly, Wilkins suggests the language event in which the learners will eventually engage as the main organizing unit for the syllabus, yet there is no clear and systematic way in which course designers could relate notions to communicative language events.

A further difficulty with the application of Wilkins' suggestions lies with the fact that often the grammatical system is not patterned along the logical lines presented in his organization of time relations. Criticism that has been launched against notional syllabuses (Brumfit 1981, Paulston 1981) has focused on the lack of systematicity that this organization results in and the fact that it does not allow for generalizations which can help learners progress from one stage to the next.

The selection of lexis in a notional syllabus will also be, at least partially, guided by the notions presented. Thus, concepts of time, quantity, and space cannot be expressed without an appropriate lexicon. Communicating emotional reactions also draws upon certain sets of lexical items. In general, however, the selection of lexis will depend on the situational content. The lexical content of a course, therefore, can be only derived from an analysis of the topics which occur in the course.

While the notional organization is inherently logical, it is not necessarily sequential. General notions such as space, time, action/event distinctions as well as more specific topics such as travel, sports, weather, occupations, etc. can be ordered in almost any sequence within the teaching materials. In fact, Trim (1984) presents an organizational model for a notional approach which takes the form of concentric discs, thus rejecting any predetermined linear sequence. However, in order to develop materials that are effective for teaching – an activity which is inherently sequential in nature – and at the same time incorporate a notional approach to organization, it may be necessary to begin by preparing carefully thought out inventories of items from which planners and developers can choose. One such inventory might contain a body of notions and semantico-grammatical categories, the second inventory would list certain functional skills needed for communication, and a third would list themes and topics to provide the context for language use. (Such inventories are discussed in chapter 6.) Materials developers would combine the elements of the three inventories according to the needs of the specific audiences for whom the program was intended.

A good language syllabus should have a well specified goal towards which all are moving; it should organize the material so that learners can constantly progress in their acquisition by using generalizations as stepping stones. It seems, therefore, that objections must give meaningful direction to the organization of learning. Yet, notions are not easily organized in a systematic manner and do not inherently lead to generalizations. One way by which developers can achieve systematicity in a notional syllabus is by mapping content within an interactive model, combining the three earlier mentioned inventories: semantico-grammatical categories, functional skills needed for communication, and themes and topics. Yet, final decisions cannot be made on the basis of the interaction of the three content inventories alone since this interaction is only one of three areas affecting the definition of communicative goals, as shown in diagram 6. Process and product need to be remapped as well before organizational decisions can be finalized.

5.1.2   Sociocultural appropriateness

A non-native speaker who is considered fluent in the language might be described by a friend as 'He's a person who speaks English very well, his grammar is really good, but sometimes he says things in a funny way.' Thus, a customer in an expensive restaurant who asks for the menu by saying, 'Waiter, we want a menu,' has produced a grammatically correct sentence, yet one that does not sound appropriate. Or similarly, a visitor in an American home who answers the offer for a cup of coffee by saying, 'Yes, of course, why do you ask?' will probably offend the hostess unintentionally. These examples illustrate the point made by Hymes (1972) that communicative competence consists of both grammatical and sociocultural rules. A person who wants to be not only linguistically correct but also socioculturally appropriate must acquire the sociocultural rules of the target language.

For a learner to acquire communicative competence in an L2 means, therefore, the acquisition of knowledge relating to linguistic form, to sociocultural appropriateness and to native preferences for certain forms rather than others. As course planners, we are faced with the gigantic task of trying to incorporate this type of knowledge into a syllabus and provide experiences that allow learners to actually use this type of knowledge. One important research area that has been expanding very rapidly in the last decade is speech act analysis. Better descriptions of speech act behavior will help planners in their decisions as to what to incorporate in language teaching materials.

Speech act theory deals with the description of the functions and uses of language, or the acts we perform through speech, thereby providing information concerning the functional component of a notional syllabus. It provides, therefore, the rules which enable speakers to choose potential linguistic forms which carry illocutionary intent. Thus a speaker of English knows that the utterance 'Can you pass me the salt?' has the illocutionary intent of a request, although its propositional meaning might relate to questioning the hearer's ability to pass the salt. Knowledge of these rules enables the speaker to produce and recognize appropriate utterances in sociocultural contexts. Ultimately, the learner will need to know in which situations it is appropriate to perform a certain speech act and which specific semantico-grammatical formula to choose in order to perform the act appropriately. (See chapter 7 for a further discussion of sociocultural appropriateness in language teaching materials.)

5.1.3 Longer spans of discourse

Discourse refers to coherent language use in particular contexts. In terms of its range, the expression refers to chunks of language which stretch beyond a single sentence. Interest in longer spans of language quite literally has expanded the content area of syllabus development during the recent period. The task of analyzing discourse entails finding the structure by which it hangs together, or makes it coherent. Just as native speakers 'know' what makes sentence sense, so are they able to recognize coherent conversations and texts, though quite likely they are unaware of why they are able to do so. Language learners also need to be able to recognize strategies which make discourse coherent.

Written and spoken discourse are distinguished from one another; written is usually planned, while spoken discourse can be planned or unplanned. Conversations, for example, are usually unplanned instances of spoken discourse. In a conversation it is difficult to predict what will be said regarding topics or procedures which keep the conversation going, yet some features of conversations are highly routinized, as is the case with openings and closings. Other examples of spoken discourse are more structured. For example, an interview is different from a conversation since it tends to contain set topics and predictable sequences. A lecture is even more planned since its topic and procedures are usually established well in advance.

Only in most recent times have teaching materials begun to incorporate content and processes which enable learners to develop conversational skills for different types of spoken discourse in the new language. Recently, research in this area has added new insights into cross-cultural elements of oral interaction, thus providing material writers with new challenges.

Analysis of written text is concerned with the discovery and description of textual structure, or texture (Halliday and Hasan 1976). Such textual features render a set of written sentences as an acceptable discourse unit, which a native speaker of that particular language recognizes as such. An important feature of such a unit is that it is cohesive, that is it maintains relations of meaning within the text linking its sentences together both structurally and logically. Cohesion is a semantic relation which is realized through the lexicogrammatical system of the language, utilizing language resources such as reference, lexical repetition, conjunction, and ellipsis, among others.

Written texts also have communicative purpose, allowing the writer to share ideas, experiences, and feelings with an audience. Another way of looking at texts is to say they have communicative potential since they can be viewed as a conversation or interaction which goes on between the writer and reader. In addition, texts contain conventional structures: narratives present stories based on chronological development of the plot; procedural texts describe processes in such a way that readers can reproduce them; and expository passages present arguments, problems and issues of a factual nature which sometimes require solutions, but at other times are descriptive in nature.

Each text type follows a conventional format, or contains discoverable, textual discourse features. Successful readers know what to expect in a particular text-type; they are able to interpret the message by utilizing organizational, lexical, and structural clues which it contains. An acceptable text, therefore, not only has cohesion, but it also has coherence, or organizational and rhetorical features which make it meaningful. 'Unity' is the term which composition teachers have traditionally given to the concept of coherence.

Focus on discourse in the context of syllabuses for second language instruction must also take in the factor of the learner's first language. The understanding that rhetorical patterns differ from one culture to another has been postulated by contrastive rhetoric (Kaplan 1966, 1972). Thus, a challenge for materials preparers is to incorporate activities which will enable L2 learner-readers to understand English discourse strategies by becoming conscious of how they accomplish reading with comprehension in their first language. One approach for writers is to incorporate into materials a variety of text types for L2 learners, thus offering them a wide spectrum through which to develop useful interpretation strategies in their reading of the new language. (See chapter 8 for a further discussion of texts and materials for teaching reading.)

5.2 Communicative processes: workouts

From the time when grammar-translation courses prevailed, through audiolingualism on into the cognitive-code period, practice material has emphasized mechanical and analytical processes. The recent communicative period has expanded this storehouse to include more global, cognitive, and creative activities as shown in diagram 6. Global activities are directed at overall language use rather than at discrete elements; cognitive activities either prepare learners for or stress intellectual aims; creative practices give learners the widest possible opportunities to use language for self-expression. Many of the global, cognitive, and creative activities that have become associated with communicative language courses have been drawn from other fields, particularly the social sciences where group interaction techniques have come in for special attention within the past decade.

The list of practice types or 'workouts' presented in 5.2.1 is meant to be open-ended. Course planners and materials writers must develop familiarity with the widest possible range, always on the lookout for ways to extend, combine, and innovate workouts. Further, they must be able to assess the suitability of a particular type for a specific objective. Moving towards establishing criteria for assessing workouts, two scales are presented in the sections 5.2.2 and 5.2.3. The first one focuses on communicative potential while the second is concerned with the cognitive area. The scales provide designers with a mechanism for providing systematicity in a syllabus through the selection of workout types. For example, a progression of workouts can be arranged in such a way to enable learners to move from less to more communicative tasks and from less to more cognitively demanding activities.

5.2.1 Workouts

Workouts are language learning and language using activities which enhance the learner's overall acquisition process, providing planners and teachers with a variety of ways through which to make this process engaging and rewarding. Samples of such workouts are presented here under ten different categories:

1. Operations/Transformations enable learners to focus on semantico-grammatical features which are necessary when aiming at accuracy in language use. All learners require such predictable and controlled workouts at times if their goal is to achieve accuracy in language production and interpretation.
2. Warm-ups/Relaxers are motivational workouts which add an element of enjoyment and personal involvement. They can be used at various points during the session, especially when a relief of tension or a change of pace is called for.
3. Information-Centered Tasks enable learners to use the language naturally while being fully engrossed in fact-gathering activities.
4. Theater Games encompass all activity types which simulate reality within the classroom situation. These workouts are especially important since they enable the language session to broaden its context beyond the four walls of the classroom.
5. Mediations/Interventions are workouts which enable learners to experience bridging information gaps while using the target language.
6, 7. Group Dynamics and Experiential Tasks are group activities which create opportunities for sharing personal feelings and emotions among learners.
8. Problem-Solving Tasks involve learners in making decisions about issues while using the target language, enabling them to focus on the features of the activity rather than on language usage. In this type of activity, learners are involved in a 'whole-task' process in Littlewood's (1981) terms.
9. While similarly 'whole-task' focused, workouts which involve transferring and reconstituting information emphasize cognitive uses of language.
10. Skill-Getting Strategies are activities which enable learners to develop specific skill areas in the target language.

Each workout type focuses on a special aspect of language use yet together they aim at helping the learner become a more effective language user.

EXAMPLE WORKOUTS:

1. *Operations/Transformations*

   For example, elements of language are added, deleted, substituted, re-ordered, or combined; alternative language elements are presented so that learners must make a choice.

2. *Warm-ups/Relaxers*

   For example, games, songs, physical activities, puzzles.

3. *Information-Centered Tasks*

   For example, share-and-tell in the classroom, gathering information outside the classroom, treasure hunts outside the classroom, interviews with peers and others.

4. *Theater Games*

   For example, improvisation (creating a scene based on a given setting or situation); role playing (assuming the role of someone else, or playing oneself in a typical situation); play enacting; story telling.

5. *Mediations/Interventions*

   For example, interacting with another or others based on incomplete information; interacting with others to change their opinions; talking one's way out of a difficult situation.

6. *Group Dynamics Activities*

   For example, small groups or pairs solve problems or discuss issues which center on topics of personal concern, sharing of self and feelings rather than general subject matter or topics external to self.

7. *Experiential Tasks*

   For example, as a group activity, making, building, constructing, or creating something concrete that relates to the thematic material of the language course.

8. *Problem-Solving Tasks*

   For example, small group discussions around topical, political or local issues; posing a concrete problem about which the group must come to a consensus, make recommendations, and arrive at a policy statement.

⟫→

9. Transferring/Reconstituting Information

For example, following a language stimulus, often a reading passage:
transferring information from text to a graphic display such as a chart;
filling in forms; providing language to complete visual displays such as
a cartoon or photograph; making judgements about people's motives and
intentions; putting sentence elements in sequence (the strip story).

10. Skill-getting Strategies

For example, in reading: previewing material before reading it, using the
SQ3R strategy (survey, question, read, recite, review); in writing:
reassembling scrambled language to build topic-sentence and paragraph
sense.

5.2.2   A scale for assessing the communicative potential of workouts:

most interactive/communicative   *least interactive*
$$1 \longleftarrow \hspace{6cm} \longrightarrow 7$$

1. New information is negotiated

Includes expression of, reaction to, and interpretation of new information.
For example, most workouts for small groups if the interaction among
members of the group is in the target language.

2. New information is expressed

For example, making up a questionnaire, writing a letter or composition,
giving an oral report, leaving a taped telephone message or a written
message, providing information to someone else.

3. New information is used or applied

For example, writing a letter in response to an advertisement, filling out
a form, answering a questionnaire which requires objective replies,
organizing main ideas in a logical sequence, strip-story activities, gathering
information outside class or from peers.

4. New information is transferred

For example, filling in a table or chart, completing a graph, putting
indicators on a map, copying information.

5. New information is received, but there is no verbal reaction

For example, communicating with a physical response, such as drawing a picture, following a route shown on a map, following instructions to construct something.

6. *No information is processed; focus is on form*

For example, mechanical operations such as ordering, combining, adding, deleting, substituting; practicing a dialogue which has been memorized; reading aloud with attention to pronunciation.

7. *New information is received (exposure only)*

For example, listening to a song, hearing a story read aloud, watching a TV program, or any extended listening period activities that do not require a physical response.

5.2.3   A scale for assessing the cognitive potential of workouts:

low		*high*
7 ←	→	1

The sequence of categories 7–1 show types of critical thinking. The examples are tasks which could be included in a language course.

1. *Evaluation*

Making a judgement of good or bad, right or wrong, valuable or useless, according to standards designated by the learner.
For example: writing a critical review of a book, play, or TV program.

2. *Synthesis*

Solving a problem that requires original, creative thinking.
For example: working with a group on a large-scale project such as planning and producing a class newsletter, a play, a panel discussion, etc.

3. *Analysis*

Solving a problem in the light of conscious knowledge of the parts and forms of thinking.
For example: playing a board game (dominoes, checkers) or a card game (gin rummy) in which choices must be made among known possibilities.

4. *Application*

Solving a life-like problem that requires the identification of the issues and the selection and use of appropriate generalizations and skills.
For example: taking part in a simulation in which the issues to be resolved are known and understood by the participants although the outcome will be determined through the group interaction itself.

⟫→

5. *Interpretation*

Discovering relationships among facts, generalizations, definitions, values, and skills.
For example: taking notes at a lecture, then using one's notes to answer evaluative questions about the content of the lecture.

6. *Translation*

Changing information into a different symbolic form or language.
For example: reading information in a text, then scanning to find specific facts in order to put the correct data in a chart, map or other graphic display.

7. *Memory*

Recalling or recognizing information.
For example: reading a passage in a text then answering comprehension questions which ask about specific details in the text.

Note: The cognitive scale was adapted from Benjamin Bloom's *Taxonomy of educational objectives* and Norris Sanders' *Classroom questions: what kinds?*

5.3   Expanded product: emphasis on skills, needs

The communicative approach has enlarged our concern with language skills, moving away from the encoding and decoding level to the use of skills for real communication.

5.3.1   Implementation of language skills

In terms of practical implementation, expansion of language skills means that learning and teaching does not stop with part-skill or contrived practice, but emphasizes instead the whole-task approach. This means that learners need to be presented with tasks which are concerned with language skills as real communication in real time, in the classroom. Similarly, the evaluation of the course product or learners' actual achievements must be done via whole-task utilization.

   The speaking skill needs to be defined in terms of the communicative use the students will be able to make of it. Such use may be quite limited for beginners or for people in courses for specialized purposes; or they may be very wide and comprehensive in scope. An example of such a limited goal might be defined as the learners' ability to ask basic questions in an interview that might be appropriate for working as a customs officer at an airport. If this is the specified goal for the students, then the activities which they carry out during the course should involve true interviewing in which they have a chance to ask real questions for which they get real answers. In the final evaluation of the course product, they should then also be given a situation in which they interview someone for real information. Alternatively, if the scope of the speaking skill is wide and comprehensive, students should experience various situations in which they actually express their own ideas and participate in true conversations and discussions. The evaluation of such overall use of the speaking skill might be carried out via roleplaying or participation in a group discussion.

The listening skill has received special attention in communicative courses, possibly because it previously had been neglected as a skill in its own right. Listening shares a number of features with reading since the two are interpretive skills which play an important role in communication. Listening, therefore, is viewed not only as the counterpart of speaking, but as an independent skill with its own objectives. In real-life, there are many situations in which we act as listeners only: as members of an audience for radio, television, lectures, films.

Courses and materials need to be created to incorporate a variety of listening activities, developing both the ability to use the skill as well as the suitable context in which to use the information gained via listening for some further application. Only by building in a need for the information to be obtained does listening become real. Here again, the evaluation of the product should be done in a fashion that resembles the activities that took place during the course.

Since communicative courses focus on the message rather than the form, the reading skill is redefined to focus on the purpose of reading. Reading fiction is not the same as reading newspaper articles; neither is like scanning the ads section for some specific information. Such varied reading objectives need to be incorporated in the course and evaluated as the desirable product at the end of it. If, for instance, the objective of a course of study has been specified as reading for general information, or getting the global picture, then students need to practice just that. If, however, learners need an overall ability to read in the new language, then interim objectives should be set out: reading narratives for the main idea, followed by reading magazine articles for general information, scanning the ad pages for specific information, and finally reading critically for factual information.

Finally, the writing skill, too, has been expanded to focus on its communicative goals. Thus, learners answer real ads in the paper, apply for jobs or write letters to their pen-pals, depending on their immediate needs for writing in the target language. In an academic course (English for academic purposes), learners write assignments appropriate to their particular field of specialization: lab reports, library research reports, etc. Writing is tied to learners' real-world needs as well: writing a resume, writing a letter seeking a job interview, writing an abstract for a professional conference presentation, etc.

Thus the writing activity becomes an interactive process with focus on 'when', 'why', and 'for what audience' writing is performed. The objective of the activity is communicating to the audience.

5.3.2   Individual needs

In chapter 1, societal needs which are significant for overall policy decisions regarding course goals were discussed. Now we are concerned with individual needs, constructing syllabus objectives with two criteria in mind: (a) the needs and wants as perceived by the particular audience in question, (b) the resources available and, accordingly, the feasibility of achieving the objectives.

Despite the attention given to course planning which emphasizes individual needs, this policy can lead to dilemmas. An assessment of individual needs could result in multiple course objectives, but in order to carry out such a plan would require resources far beyond those which are available. Therefore, course designers must make adjustments and look for needs which actually reflect the majority in a given learner population rather than actual individuals. Also, designing courses in terms of individual needs is problematic when plans must be set for groups in advance of their arrival at a particular instructional setting. Needs, too, can be interpreted differently by different members of the audience for courses and materials. Thus students can perceive needs in one way while faculty or even specialized faculty, for example the language faculty, assess needs differently. These real-world variables inevitably mean that planning becomes an activity based not only on data from fact-finding instruments but also on experience with previous groups, and on the experiential process developing within the course itself.

5.3.3   Learner autonomy – an added product

Contemporary courses based on a humanistic view of teaching often place emphasis on the development of learner autonomy as the major objective of the syllabus. Success of the course and level of achievement on the part of the students is not measured by how much the students know at the end of the course or by what they can do with language, but rather by how independent they have become as language learners. A course that is so designed must allow for considerable student-student interaction, and must provide learners with ample material resources. Students are expected to take full advantage of what is available and make decisions as to what topics and what activities they want to carry out. The teacher plays the role of an evaluator and observer in assessing to what extent learners have become independent. Sometimes the final course activity is an independent or group project and the evaluation of success is carried out jointly by teacher and student. Examples might be art, music, or writing projects which the students create and execute on their own: a group paints an outdoor mural; a group produces an end-of-school-year musical play; a group writes a class almanac.

5.3.4 Highlighting particular syllabus components

In planning courses, designers need to work with all three expanded areas: language content, process and product. In some instances, however, the product area might take precedence; for example, in a course aimed entirely at reading comprehension, the reading skill would be of primary significance, while the other areas – content and process – would be organized so as to serve the overall reading goals. Systematicity of organization would be achieved by planning a progression which facilitates the acquisition and development of good reading strategies. Learner autonomy, in this case, would be realized in the form of the learners' selection of reading matter according to their own choices. The course designers would allow learners to set up their own reading objectives, encouraging them to evaluate their own progress in becoming effective readers. In this way, learner autonomy would be an integral part of the expected outcomes of such a course.

In contrast to one focused on reading as a single goal, another course might aim at overall proficiency. Learners who take a foreign language as part of their school program often have such an open and general objective. In this case, motivation and interest in the target language become significant goals of the program; they are independent of the actual achievements in language use. Course content becomes, therefore, of primary importance. The learners need to become involved in interesting themes and exciting tasks while learning and using the language within the classroom situation. The systematic organization of the course, in this case, might be derived from a thematic approach. Themes/topics would be selected and sequenced according to the learners' interests and background knowledge, while lexis, semantico-grammatical features, and communicative functions would be selected to serve the treatment of each theme. Further, tasks/workouts would be placed in a sequence according to the scales which were suggested earlier in this chapter, while all language skills would be utilized in an integrated manner within each thematic unit.

Practical applications

I   ASSESS AND ILLUSTRATE WORKOUTS:

1. Assess each category in the list of workouts (section 5.2.1) according to whether it stresses one or more of these areas: mechanical, analytical, global, cognitive, creative.
2. Find examples of five of the types of workouts listed in section 5.2.1 in published textbooks. Assess the textbooks in terms of the variety of workouts which appear in each.
3. Assess the workout types you have found according to the two scales, for communicative and cognitive potential. What other kinds of scales do course designers need to work with?
4. As a group activity, construct a scale that would assess the creative potential of workouts.
5. In the examples for the cognitive scale (section 5.2.3), add at least one additional task to illustrate each category in the scale.
6. For further reading on evaluating practice types (workouts), see Stevick (1971), chapter 3.

2   PLAN A NEW COURSE:

In a group, undertake the task of planning a two-months, intensive English course for a group of twenty adults (ages 25–35) from a non-European language background. Choose whether the course takes place in the country of origin (in an EFL setting) or whether the students have just arrived in an English speaking country and will be taking the course in an ESL setting.

The learners are to be sent by a multinational company to act as trade representatives in English speaking countries. The overall goal for them is to achieve a high level of oral proficiency in English by the end of the two-months course. All you know about the English language competence of the participants is that they have all completed a six-year EFL course of study in secondary school and are able to communicate in faulty, non-fluent English. Some have had English courses at the university level. Their reading proficiency is rather good and they read authentic English material both for pleasure and for professional needs. During the two months intended for the course, they will have 8–10 hours a day available for English studies, including work in a language laboratory, some use of computers, and ample materials in a self-access center. They are most willing to take part in cultural and other events in which the English language dominates, if these are available.

The group's task is:

1. To set up a list of objectives for each of the three expanded areas of the syllabus: language content, process/means, and product/outcomes.

2. To decide on a daily schedule which all learners can be involved in, taking into consideration questions of fatigue and boredom on the one hand and availability of a variety of equipment on the other. (Make use of the language setting which you have selected – ESL or EFL.)
3. To show how a unit of materials could be created making use of the language content inventories discussed in chapter 5.

References

Bloom, B. S. (Ed.) 1956. *Taxonomy of educational objectives*. New York: David McKay Co. Inc.

Brumfit, C. J. 1981. 'Notional syllabuses revisited: a response'. *Applied Linguistics* II (1), pp. 90–3.

Halliday, M. A. K. and R. Hasan. 1976. *Cohesion in English*. London: Longman.

Hymes, D. H. 1972. 'On communicative competence'. In J. B. Pride and J. Holmes (Eds.) *Sociolinguistics*. Harmondsworth: Penguin Books.

Kaplan, R. 1966. 'Cultural thought patterns in intercultural education'. *Language Learning* 16, 1–2, pp. 1–20.

Kaplan, R. 1972. 'The anatomy of rhetoric'. In R. C. Lugton (Ed.) *English as a second language: current issues*. Philadelphia: Center for Curriculum Development.

Littlewood, W. 1981. *Communicative language teaching*. Cambridge: Cambridge University Press.

Paulston, C. B. 1981. 'Notional syllabuses revisited: some comments'. *Applied Linguistics* II (1), pp. 93–6.

Roget's Thesaurus (Ed. S. M. Lloyd) 1982. Harlow: Longman.

Sanders, N. 1966. *Classroom questions: what kinds?* New York: Harper and Row.

Stevick, E. 1971. *Adapting and writing language lessons*. Washington, D.C. Foreign Service Institute. (Superintendent of Documents, U.S. Govt Printing Office, 20402.)

Trim, J. L. M. 1984. Extract from 'Developing a unit/credit scheme of adult language learning'. In J. A. van Ek and J. L. M. Trim (Eds.) *Across the threshold*. Oxford: Pergamon Press.

Wilkins, D. A. 1976. *Notional syllabuses*. Oxford: Oxford University Press.

Wilkins, D. A. 1981. 'Notional syllabuses revisited: a further reply'. *Applied Linguistics* II (1), pp. 96–100.

Other suggested readings

Hymes, D. H. 1964. 'Toward ethnographies of communication'. In J. J. Gumperz and D. H. Hymes (Eds.) 'The ethnography of communication'. Special issue: *American Anthropologist* 66 (6) part 2, pp. 1–34.

6 Focusing on language content in a communicative syllabus

Overview

In a communicative syllabus, the language content dimension has expanded to include notional and functional meaning along with structures, situations, and themes (see diagram 6). In section 6.1, *Integrating notional and functional meaning with grammar, thematic content, and lexis,* suggestions are presented on how to integrate the various elements of the expanded content of a communicative syllabus. What is needed is to develop separate inventories of forms, notions, functions, themes and lexis for a particular audience. In section 6.2, *Discrete and holistic views: the horns of a dilemma,* it is pointed out that the dilemma exists in all three of the dimensions of a syllabus: language content, process, and product. Further, this dilemma has implications which go far beyond the field of language pedagogy.

6.1 Integrating notional and functional meaning with grammar, thematic content and lexis

A major difficulty in syllabus design is the fact that learning a language cannot be explained as learning single units of any kind, be they notions, functions, structures, or lexis. It is some combination of all these together, along with the previous experience that the learner brings to the task, which accounts for language learning. ESL/EFL learners already possess a solid knowledge of notions, functions, and lexis which underlie their first language. What seems important to teach, therefore, as Rivers (1980) points out are the interlingual contrasts between the notions in L1 and the target language.

The idea of gender, for example, may be understood both by a speaker of English and a speaker of French, yet the way gender is used in these two languages is so very different that learners from both backgrounds have difficulties adjusting to the system used in another language. The information about how the new language works is significant and cannot be taken lightly in designing the course. This is true even if the student's ultimate goal for the course of study is not perfect accuracy in the new language but only interpretive ability.

Similarly, the way time is marked in a language by the tense system may be different enough to cause difficulty for the learner. In English, for instance, there is a basic, comprehensive distinction between actions and events viewed internally as having a beginning, middle, and end (durative or progressive), and events or actions perceived in their totality (non-progressive). Speakers of another language who understand the basic notions of time and duration will have difficulty with the English aspect system if their language does not make significant, marked distinctions between durative and non-durative. Here, again, this distinction relates not only to expressing oneself in language, but also to interpreting language produced by others. As Rivers (1980:53) claims: '... much more attention should be paid in classroom teaching to the comprehensive and thorough assimilation of these fundamental conceptual differences between languages so that students are learning to operate within the total language system, rather than picking up minor skills in its application.'

The state of the art seems to be such that there is an immediate necessity to 'find new ways of teaching form and use together' (Eskey 1983). Course designers need to do the following:
1. Present linguistic forms systematically to enable learners to express the basic notions of language. Furthermore, special emphasis needs to be placed on interlingual differences relating to the realization of notions.
2. Use communicative context to allow learners to interact within a wide range of communicative language functions. Here again, emphasis must be placed on sociocultural language specific features in order to produce utterances which are appropriate to the cultural setting. Among the many possible choices available for expressing functions, materials must begin with those which are highly frequent in native speech and only gradually expand to include the less frequent ones (Canale and Swain 1980).
3. Use a variety of text-types both in the oral and written form in order to develop communicative proficiency in all language skills, unless a specific course calls for emphasis on one or two language skills rather than on all.

6.1.1 *Developing inventories*

Ideally, what is needed for course development is to combine forms, notions, functions, lexis and language skills. At first glance this seems a rather impossible task, but if we develop useful inventories for a particular audience in each of these areas, then it should become feasible.

I.   INVENTORY A: NOTIONS AND GRAMMAR

Inventory A consists of two separate lists: (a) All the grammatical topics to be taught during the course, organized in a sequence suitable for systematic learning and for generalizations that can be developed along the way. (b) A list of notional categories to be taught during the course. These two separate lists are then combined into units comprising notions and structures in a way that allows us to show how notional categories and grammatical categories interact. Careful preparatory work has to be done by the course planners themselves. They can, of course, use examples such as the Threshold Level (van Ek 1977) for the notional lists and any good grammar for the grammatical categories. The combination, however, will have to be developed for the particular course and will require a number of planning and conceptualization sessions before worthwhile lists can be produced.

As an example of a combined teaching unit of notions and grammar, consider the notion time and its interaction with the tense-aspect system in English. This unit has to be broken down into teachable portions which may have to spread throughout the course, creating a type of spiralling plan where the unit of time and tense-aspect recurs with expanded topics every few weeks or so. Thus the planners might decide that the most logical place to begin this unit is with the durative aspect which in English is probably different from all other languages, requiring special focus in the materials.

Alternatively, planners may decide to begin with a description of time-less, static statements such as factual information, routine activities and the like which are non-durative. The decisions on sequence will be based on both linguistic generalizations, similarity, difference for L1, and other didactic variables such as the teachers' abilities to provide examples and contexts for the particular topic, availability of such a relevant context in the immediate environment, and other similar considerations. The important point is that by working with combined units of notions and structures, designers should be able to ensure the inclusion of both types of categories throughout the syllabus. Furthermore, the spiralling approach will enable teachers and learners to tackle difficult areas again and again, at different levels of sophistication and within different contextual situations.

Inventory A provides the skeleton of the program, the backbone around which other elements will have to be developed using Inventories B and C (discussed below). Moreover, basic considerations of sequencing in course planning cannot be thrown out entirely, despite what some curriculum designers believed in the early days of the communicative approach. As Brumfit (1981) states, '... a syllabus implies movement, it must contain a starting point as well as an end point.'

108

2. INVENTORY B: THEMES AND TOPICS

Inventory B is a list of themes and topics. Its main purpose is twofold: (a) To provide appropriate cultural contextualization for the language material in the syllabus, and (b) to motivate interest by using topics that are relevant and appealing to a particular group of learners. This inventory is of vital importance and may ultimately make or break the course in terms of its success in the classroom. The topics to be included may come from questionnaires administered to potential students of similar age groups and interests as well as from open discussions with students at a similar level.

Another strategy for topic selection is to integrate content from other subject matter areas in the course curriculum. For example, major topics that appear in history, geography, social studies, or science can be integrated with the English language course by using them in the specification of themes and topics. In the language pedagogy literature, this approach has been called 'language in the content area'. A related suggestion in ESL in higher education is the 'sheltered course' in which non-native students learn the English language through special classes in subject content areas: for example history and economics.

3. INVENTORY C: SOCIOCULTURAL FUNCTIONS

Inventory C is a list of communicative, sociocultural functions which the planners decide to include in the course of study. However, planners are faced with serious difficulties since there is no reference text that provides a comprehensive description of speech act behavior in English much less for the first languages of the learners. What designers would need to know from such a reference text would be the following information about each speech act that they decide to include in the course plan:

1. The typical situations in which each speech act is used by native speakers. For example, what are some typical situations in which native speakers of English tend to apologize, complain, or compliment the hearer?
2. The extent to which the speech act changes in form or selection of the particular utterance according to the participants taking part.
3. The most frequent utterances that native speakers use to carry out this speech act in formal and informal settings.

Sociolinguistic research seems to be a long way from having comprehensive answers to these questions. Since planning and developing language courses is required for use now, designers may have to consult their intuitions about these matters or consult with native speakers, if they are not themselves speakers of the TL. What is important, however, is that planners try to look for answers to these questions before embarking on incorporating speech acts into materials. Too many recent texts have devoted long pages to 'making suggestions' or 'giving advice', randomly listing dated or infrequently used forms along with useful ones. But learners have no way of distinguishing among them; moreover, such units often contain endless lists of options when learners have no tools or criteria for making choices the way native speakers do. Although there are no perfect answers today on speech act behavior, by trying to answer the above three questions for every speech act that is included in a syllabus, designers may be able to come up with more useful materials.

4.   COMBINING THE THREE INVENTORIES

The most difficult task in focus selection is combining the three inventories. The goal is to create course plans which will consist of a theme (including related sub-topics), a list of notions and grammatical structures, and a selection of functions. The first concern is: which inventory should be the basic one? Here the answer depends entirely on course goals: the linguistic inventory has traditionally been organized in a certain sequence so it fits everyone's cultural expectations. Like reciting the alphabet in customary order, it seems natural and basic. One could still begin with the linguistic inventory and build around it. This is not imperative, however. One could just as easily select another inventory to begin with. Inventories B and C, however, do not require any inherent sequential ordering. It seems easy, therefore, to use Inventory A for skeletal planning and then provide the padding and the flesh of the units from Inventories B and C.

Assume the designers decide to focus on verb phrases that express habitual, regular events (non-durative present) under the general notion time with special focus on frequency, information which comes from Inventory A. Picking up Inventory B, they now look for a theme or topic that could provide this notional-grammatical unit with suitable contextual background. There are various possibilities, depending on the age and background of students, issues of current relevance, etc. For example, assume they choose the topic of travel and within it focus on modern means of transportation. When merging Inventory A with B (travel-transportation with time/aspect) they come up against a few additional difficulties. For one, once they have made the theme/topic decision in their selection, to a great extent, additional decisions will now be guided by it.

The planners working with this unit may realize the need to add adjectives and modals based on their experience with a particular learner audience. Or, they may decide to add them to encourage learners to use these structures. What is important is that these structural elements should not occur in isolation, devoid of meaning. Rather, all structure-focused activities should be used to provide additional communicative practice around the theme of transportation-travel.

The planners could, however, start with Inventory B as the focal skeleton. Doing so would suit a thematic organizational design. Assume that one of the general themes is 'food and drink'. A number of sub-themes or topics would be listed within this general theme such as: shopping for food and drinks, eating habits in different places in the world, eating out, health foods, diet foods, food exports and imports, exotic fruit, etc. Of course, many other possible topics could be added to the list to suit a particular learner audience for which the course is being planned.

Each sub-theme would then be expanded to relate to certain functions: in the unit on shopping, the learners would need to ask for information concerning prices, quantities, brands, sizes, etc. When discussing exports, they may want to interview an expert on the topic which would lead to the inclusion of functions such as introductions, invitations, requests, suggestions, expressions of agreement, etc. These functions would then make up Inventory C for this thematic unit. Finally, the planners would come back to Inventory A and select various grammatical features needed in order to deal with the various sub-themes and functions. Thus, for example, for the shopping sub-theme they may need quantifiers for the different types of food and drink and mastery of the question mechanism in order to ask for information.

Whether the planners choose to begin with Inventory A, B, or C as the pivotal core of the course will depend entirely on the goals and the audiences they have in mind. An example of such an interaction of different inventories is found in the planning 'map' for Swan and Walter's (1984) *The Cambridge English Course* (see overleaf).

6.1.2 The choice of lexis

In merging Inventories A and B, an issue arises that has not been discussed so far, namely the choice of lexis or the stock of vocabulary items. This merger is a crucial step since from it decisions are made within the thematic unit concerning the lexical items to be included. These lexical decisions must override other considerations, giving lexis the proper emphasis and suitable focus it richly deserves within the thematic unit, otherwise learners may not be able to take full advantage of the elements of the theme.

In course designing, lexis is derived in part from the notional-grammatical inventory (time expressions, prepositions, verbs that fit the patterns which have been included etc.), but more significantly it is drawn from the thematic content. Lexis has failed to receive enough attention either

Illustration 6.1

Map of Book 1*

In Unit	Students will learn to	Students will learn to talk about
1	Ask and give names; say hello; ask and tell where people are from.	Numbers.
2	Say hello formally and informally; ask about and give personal information.	Jobs; age.
3	Describe people; tell the time.	Family relationships.
4	Describe places; give compliments; express uncertainty; confirm and correct information.	Geography; numbers to 1,000,000.
5	Describe houses and flats; make and answer telephone calls.	Home: furniture, addresses; telephones.
6	Express likes and dislikes; ask about and describe habits and routines.	Habits and routines.
7	Ask and tell about quantity.	Food and drink; shopping; quantification.
8	Ask for and give directions; ask and tell about physical and emotional states.	Finding your way in a town.
9	Express degrees of certainty; talk about frequency.	How people live; how animals live; weather and climate.
10	Describe people's appearances; give compliments; write simple letters.	Colours; parts of the body; clothing; resemblances.
REVISION	Use what they have learnt in different ways.	Physical description.

Michael Swan and Catherine Walter, *Cambridge English Course 1* © 1984, Cambridge University Press

in older grammatical syllabuses or in more recent communicative approaches. In fact, lay people believe that 'knowing a language' consists of knowing words, while modern linguistic theories have placed little emphasis on vocabulary, focusing more on structures, functions, notions, and communicative strategies. However, it may be the case that possessing a good vocabulary stock is what enables many learners to use their knowledge of the language effectively and in ways which fit their specific needs.

By using the inventory system, designers are able to choose new lexical items which draw on the selected theme. As a result, semantically related words can be presented in varied contexts, all deriving from that theme. Then, when learners come across unfamiliar words they are able to make hypotheses about their meanings which they can realistically test. In this way, the lexical content forms the input upon which learners work. But input alone is far from sufficient. The next task is for materials writers to produce effective workouts for classroom practice which foster the mastery of new lexical items.

6.2   Discrete and holistic views: the horns of a dilemma

In constructing inventories with which to integrate the various components of language content, course planners come to grips with a dilemma which has the broadest possible ramifications. For it is paradoxical that although language is experienced comprehensively, in order to specify what goes into our syllabuses and course outlines, we have had to rely on analyses which dissect it into bits and pieces. The cause for this is

Students will learn these grammar points	Students will study these aspects of pronunciation
Present of *to be* (singular); possessive adjectives.	Word-stress; weak forms.
A/an with jobs; subject pronouns.	Rhythm; intonation; linking; stress pattern recognition.
Noun plurals; *'s* for possession; present of *to be* (plural); *have got*; adjectives; adverbs of degree.	/ð/; *o* in *mother*, etc.; stress; intonation; linking /r/.
A/an contrasted with *the*; adjectives before nouns; *on/in/at* with places; *Isn't that...?*	/θ/ and /ð/; /ðə/ and /ði:/; word-stress and resultant /ə/; intonation of answers; intonation for contrast; linking.
There is/there are; simple present affirmative, *this/that*; *Can/Could I...?*; *tell* + object + *that*-clause; formation of noun plurals.	Weak forms; linking and rhythm with *there is/there are*; contrastive stress; rising and falling intonation; plural endings.
Simple Present; omission of article; *like* + -*ing*; *neither... nor*; object pronouns; *at* with times; *by* (*bus*); *from... until*.	Stress and rhythm; decoding fast speech.
Countables and uncountables; expressions of quantity; omission of article; *was/were*; *some* and *any*; *much* and *many*.	Word-stress; weak forms.
For + expressions of distance; *to be* with *hungry*, *thirsty*, etc.	Intonation of polite questions; stress and rhythm; weak form of *at*.
Complex sentences; text building; frequency adverbs; impersonal *it*.	Stress and /ə/; /i:/ and /ɪ/.
Have got; *both* and *all*; *look like*; *What (a)...!*	
(Revision) *Be* contrasted with *have*; *there is/there are*; questions with noun-phrase subjects.	Perceiving weak forms and unstressed words; /θ/ and /ð/; intonation; pronunciation of words with misleading spellings.

a practical one. Planners need to work with maps of language content which are compatible with the chronological constraints of the instructional setting, so grammars which segment language into discrete elements have great appeal. However, when the goals of the course are deemed to be communicative competence, or any aspect of it, then opposite ends seem to be pulling at each other. The realization of this dilemma brings into focus two separate ways of looking at human language: the discrete and the holistic.

6.2.1 The holistic view

The holistic view has been in the limelight in the recent, communicative period with three distinct strands contributing to its upturn. First, it has gained prominence through the influence of a humanistically-oriented philosophy of education in which the development of the whole person is stressed. This view emphasizes the total individual and his/her needs for using language as the basic goal to be met by the curriculum. Second, the unit of analysis of language itself has come to be viewed by linguistic scholars and those in related disciplines not as a single sentence, but rather as longer spans of language or discourse. As Widdowson (1978b:22) explains: We must move away from only considering facts about single sentences or words (language usage) to considering how language works in a communicative sense (language use) 'this requires us to go beyond the sentence and to look at longer stretches of language.'

A third influence which has brought holistic practices into wide acceptance can be traced to the influence of mother-tongue instruction, or the language arts field typified by practices which foster language development in young children: reading aloud to children by adults; learning center activities; language experience activities; child-authored stories; individual reading and re-telling; simulating real-life through activities such as letter writing, making stationery, writing lists, taking messages, designing greeting cards, writing notes to friends, etc. These practices seem 'right' to teachers because they come closer to real communication. However, they go against specialists' ideas of what is exact or precise because they fail to include discrete analyses of language.

6.2.2   The discrete view

In contrast, second and foreign language instruction has, to a great extent, incorporated the discrete element view of language, particularly in audiolingual and cognitive-code approaches. Even in the recent period, whether the content has been grammatical structures or semantic concepts expressed as notions, we have relied on analyses of language in constructing inventories which depend for their discovery procedures on processes of dissecting and segmenting into elements. In linguistic science these discrete entities are given names such as 'phonemes', 'morphemes', and 'sentences'. When we work with illocutionary meaning, speech acts, or functions in language, we tend to seek ways of putting such elements into similar categories. Moreover, the fact that we lack reference texts which describe language functions leaves us feeling dissatisfied. It may turn out, however, that our quests for 'grammars' of social interaction based on building-block units tend to reflect our deeply imbued western cultural tradition which has been based on discovering particles since the seventeenth century when a conceptual framework for science – built around the model proclaimed for physics – was developed based on the mathematical theory of Isaac Newton, the philosophy of René Descartes, and the scientific methodology advocated by Francis Bacon.

6.2.3   Evidence of the discrete vs. holistic paradox in language content, process, and product

The discrete vs. holistic paradox appears in each of the dimensions of an idealized syllabus. As diagram 7 indicates, each of the areas, language content, process, and product can be viewed both from a discrete and from a holistic point of view, creating a continuum with the discrete perspective on the one end and the holistic perspective on the other. The discrete point of view focuses on form, accuracy and analysis while the holistic point focuses on function, fluency, and use. Moreover, in each area there is an element of opposition which seems to keep the two points in tension.

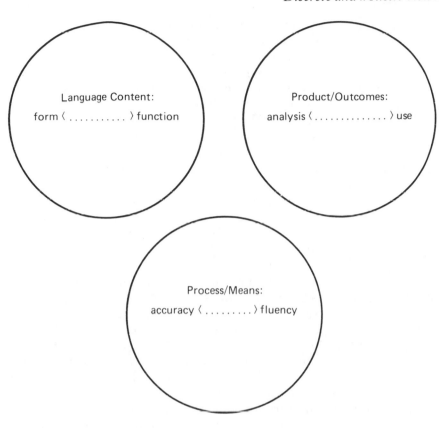

Diagram 7   The discrete vs. holistic paradox

I.   FORM AND FUNCTION

The dichotomy between formal patterns in language and 'types of concepts' that make up their meaning (Sapir 1921), or grammatical form as distinct from function, has been accepted as a basic understanding about the nature of language for a very long time, enabling people who work with it to be able to separate formal, grammatical properties from aspects of meaning, including notions and functions. Also from Sapir's writings, we understand that human languages differ in the manner in which forms represent functions. Moreover, structural forms and functions in a language are rarely if ever isomorphic, occurring in the same shape. In the way we have used the term, language content includes both formal properties (grammar) and all types of meaning (notions, functions, social norms for use, etc.). Further, forms and functions in

115

language are themselves manifestations of the discrete vs. holistic dilemma as it appears in the domain of language content.

Within language content, the discrete vs. holistic phenomena can be set out on a scale reflecting our present conceptual ability to deal with these seemingly opposite poles. On the discrete end is grammar, which traditionally we regard as segmentable. In fact, linguists in the structural period, anxious to legitimize the field as 'scientific', claimed that unlike the data used in the social sciences, the data with which linguistics deals can be analyzed for their smallest, inherent properties. Therefore, linguistics was more closely akin to the hard sciences.

Notions, too, turn out to be classifiable; although the tradition of analysis is nowhere near as finely developed as is that of grammar. That notions belong somewhere on the scale closer to discrete than to holistic was brought to our attention when Wilkins' notional syllabus was criticized for being 'an inventory of units, of items for accumulation and storage' (Widdowson 1978a).

Less amenable to description as units are language functions, at least when the quest is for classifiable entities such as speech acts: complaining, apologizing, promising, requesting, reporting, and several hundred others. Although speech acts are describable in broad, philosophic terms (Searle 1969), we do not have maps of their organizational features, or answers to the three questions stated earlier in this chapter in section 6.1., (3) Inventory C. However, an international cross-cultural study of speech act realization patterns (Blum-Kulka and Olshtain 1984) is trying to find such answers for a number of languages. On the other hand, topical and thematic approaches to organizing language instruction appear to be quite holistic, composed as they are of stuff which does not lend itself to being set out in any kind of sequential fashion, based on criteria of internal organization.

2.   ACCURACY AND FLUENCY

In the domain of process, the discrete vs. holistic quandary is manifested through the opposites of accuracy and fluency (Brumfit 1979, Eskey 1983). So, procedures for instruction which stress mastery of discrete elements have been called accuracy practices or stress on 'rules' of language content. Fluency, on the other hand, has been associated with communicating one's idea, getting the meaning across, or in the terms of the dichotomy, using language either holistically or comprehensively.

But the issue appears to be more complex. Accuracy processes, as we think of them at the present, for the most part are concerned with those aspects of language content that are conducive to analysis through dissection. Holistic processes, on the other hand, hold out the promise of drawing on ways to look at language which are instead based on

116

larger, more complex systems. But it is a mistake to assume that all fluency workouts fail to consider the systematic properties of language. It is possible to create holistic workouts which attend to cultural and social norms that are outside the language code, but which still focus on communicative characteristics of the target language. For example, learners of English who need to be culturally prepared for the dynamics of a job interview either in the United States or the United Kingdom can watch videotapes contrasting native and non-native job seekers being interviewed. Afterwards, the contrastive features are pointed out and discussed including such points as the kinds of questions asked, the kinds of replies given, the non-verbal characteristics of both interviewer and job-seeker, etc.

3.   ANALYSIS AND USE

The holistic vs. discrete dichotomy appears in the domain of product/outcomes as the fluctuation between courses which have emphasized analysis and those which have emphasized use, particularly when viewed historically (see chapter 2, section 2.1.4). Or, as the concept has been personified recently (Rivers 1981), the dichotomy which exists between the views of 'formalists', those who stress knowing the formal properties of language as a proper outcome for learners in a language course, and 'activists', those who stress using language actively.

6.2.4   *Reconciling opposites in the instructional plans*

Faced with the dilemma of integrating discrete elements or analyses of language content with holistic, comprehensive use of it, various sequential plans have been proposed for course designs:

1. A holistic approach is adopted with emphasis on thematic, meaningful interaction which is self-motivating. In addition to holistic language experiences for the whole group, there are workbooks for use by individuals which concentrate on grammatical points and specific skills.
2. A more structural/notional approach is adopted in the syllabus with emphasis on the skills that have been selected as most important for the course. To meet individual needs, other materials are in use in a learning center or a language laboratory in which there is emphasis on thematic and communicative use of language.
3. The early phase of the course is structural. Later, as learners progress in their basic acquisition of grammatical competence, they move on to a more holistic approach, utilizing global language in communicative workouts.
4. The course follows a thematic, communicative tone, similar to a lan-

guage arts course for native-speaker children. At a later stage, more attention is given to accuracy and form. In this instance, Gestalt learning comes first and discrete-point elements are added later.

Which of these designs seems to be suitable will depend on the particular situation and the group of students. However, writers who must plan for large numbers of learners, for example people who write textbook series, are faced with serious questions which, if they are to be successfully answered, require a great deal of keen intuition, skill, plus a bit of luck at balancing trends in the field with topical interests and outlooks which will appeal to a maximally general audience.

6.2.5 Other systems, other worlds

Are there additional ways to analyze language that advance the discussion beyond the issue of the discrete vs. the holistic? Are there other glasses we might try on through which to perceive things from another perspective? Materials writers who want to shed the constraints of discrete point analyses, yet who realize that language content for course design purposes must be based on some kind of orderly presentation, would do well to look to other fields that study human language as a communication process. What are the complex systems of language which other social sciences have determined? An interesting tip of the iceberg is mentioned by Morrow (1981:62) regarding 'information gaps', a concept that comes from communication theory. From this source we realize that our materials might incorporate, through workouts, ways which get learners to use language holistically by seeking withheld information with which to successfully accomplish a given task.

Other suggestions have been made for the utilization of language content based on analyses that are less tied to discreteness since they draw on systemic characteristics. As already mentioned, from the field of philosophy the communicative approach has incorporated speech act theory, a way of looking at categories of language use which relies more on complex relationships than on discrete elements.

From the field of ethnomethodology have come significant insights into how users employ language to carry out their everyday, mundane business. For example, ethnomethodologists have described how people take turns in conversation, how they organize their speaking in relation to each other, how they punctuate their talk through employing tactics for signaling openings and closings, startings and breaking-off points (Schegloff 1968, Sacks 1972). The starting point for ethnomethodology is not language, *per se*, but rather the constructs of sociology: norms, values, roles, interest coalitions, and the like.

While grappling with the discrete point vs. holistic dilemma in our work as course designers and materials writers, we recognize, too, that the question has a much larger scope. When we take a moment off to poke our heads outside our own cave, we note that the issue shows up in many of the disciplines which western science pursues. From physics to biology to geology, and in other related areas, the dilemma is a central theoretical issue of recent time. Traditionally, western science has been largely influenced by a Cartesian view which 'believed that complex phenomena could always be understood by reducing them to their basic building blocks and by looking at the mechanisms through which these interacted. This attitude, known as reductionism, has become so deeply ingrained in our culture that it has often been identified with the scientific method' (Capra 1982: 47).

Capra goes on to point out that 'in the twentieth century ... the universe is no longer seen as a machine, made up of a multitude of separate objects, but appears as a harmonious indivisible whole; a network of dynamic relationships that include the human observer and his or her consciousness in an essential way.'

Such an approach to the study of human language might provide course designers a framework which brings about a synthesis of discrete and holistic views.

Practical applications

1. In planning the unit discussed in section 6.1.1, what lexical items could be included given the thematic content which has been selected (transportation-travel)? To answer this question you should first specify a particular audience in terms of age, general education level, language background, together with any other information which specifies the setting for which the course plan is being developed.
2. The next step after determining the lexical items to be included is to add elements from Inventory C, or communicative functions. Working with the same thematic content and structural forms already mentioned, what functions would be suitable?
3. Using the same audience and course plan you selected for questions 1 and 2, what language skills would be suitable? Remember, first you must determine if the plan is directed to all skills (an integrative approach), or to specialized skill needs.
4. For further explorations of notional and semantic categories in course planning, see Johnson (1982) and Yalden (1983).

6   *Focusing on language content in a communicative syllabus*

References

Blum-Kulka, S. and E. Olshtain, 1984. 'Requests and apologies: a cross-cultural study of speech act realization patterns'. *Applied Linguistics* V(3), pp. 196–214.
Brumfit, C. J. 1979. '"Communicative" language teaching: an educational perspective'. In C. J. Brumfit and K. Johnson (Eds.) *The communicative approach to language teaching,* pp. 183–91. Oxford: Oxford University Press.
Brumfit, C. J. 1981. 'Notional syllabuses revisited: a response'. *Applied Linguistics* II(1), pp. 90–3.
Canale, M. and M. Swain. 1980. 'Theoretical bases of communicative approaches to second language teaching and testing'. *Applied Linguistics* I(1), pp. 1–47.
Capra, F. 1982. *The turning point.* New York: Simon and Schuster.
van Ek, J. A. 1977. *The threshold level for modern language learning in schools.* London: Longman.
Eskey, D. E. 1983. 'Meanwhile back in the real world . . . accuracy and fluency in second language teaching'. *TESOL Quarterly* 17(2), pp. 315–23.
Johnson, K. 1982. *Communicative syllabus design and methodology.* Oxford: Pergamon Press.
Morrow, K. 1981. 'Principles of communicative methodology'. In K. Johnson and K. Morrow (Eds.) *Communication in the classroom,* pp. 59–69. Harlow: Longman.
Rivers, W. 1980. 'Foreign language acquisition: where the real problems lie'. *Applied Linguistics* I(1), pp. 48–59.
Rivers W. 1981. *Teaching foreign-language skills.* Second edition. Chicago: Chicago University Press.
Sacks, H. 1972. 'An initial investigation of the usability of conversational data for doing sociology'. In D. Sudnow (Ed.) *Studies in social interaction,* pp. 31–74. New York: The Free Press.
Sapir, E. 1921. *Language, an introduction to the study of speech.* New York: Harcourt, Brace and World. (Harvest Books).
Schegloff, E. A. 1968. 'Sequencing in conversational openings'. *American Anthropologist* 70, pp. 1075–95.
Searle, J. R. 1969. *Speech acts. An essay in the philosophy of language.* New York: Cambridge University Press.
Swan, M. and C. Walter. 1984. *The Cambridge English Course, Student's Book 1.* Cambridge: Cambridge University Press.
Widdowson, H. G. 1978a. 'Notional-functional syllabuses: 1978'. In C. Blatchford and J. Schachter (Eds.) *On TESOL '78: EFL policies, programs, practices,* pp. 33–5. Washington, D.C.: TESOL.
Widdowson H. G. 1978b. *Teaching language as communication.* Oxford: Oxford University Press.
Yalden, J. 1983. *The communicative syllabus: evolution, design, and implementation.* Oxford: Pergamon Press.

Other suggested readings

Wilkins, D. A. 1981. 'Notional syllabuses revisited: a further reply'. *Applied Linguistics* II(1), pp. 96–100.

7 Focusing on process: materials that deal with sociocultural appropriateness

Overview

In chapter 7 and those following, the focus shifts to materials preparation. The purpose in these chapters is not to present an encyclopedic coverage of all possible types, but rather to show how effective materials writing draws, first of all, on a thorough understanding of the nature of language, in both its spoken and written forms.

When communicative competence has been determined as a curriculum goal, writers look for ways to include the sociocultural component of language content, or so-called rules of appropriateness, in the materials they create. As will be shown in section 7.1, *Incorporating grammars of social norms: a discrete element view*, the issues for writers are vexing, the state of the art very young. In fact, the link between workout types and sociocultural content has barely begun to be explored. Dealing with social norms in language may be better suited, however, to holistic processes than to focusing on discrete elements. One such holistic workout type, the roleplay, is carefully examined in section 7.2, *Scripting roleplays: a holistic view of sociocultural content*.

7.1 Incorporating grammars of social norms: a discrete element view

With language content expanded to include sociocultural matter as well as grammatical form, writers are challenged to find modes for incorporating it in materials. In doing so, they face some compelling issues. For example, when, why, and how should we deal with sociolinguistic aspects? Are rules of social appropriateness necessary for all courses? What content needs to be explicitly included? Should rules of sociocultural interaction be presented sequentially, one step at a time as has grammar?

Effective writing demands that the language in either a commercial textbook or teacher-prepared materials embody basic sociolinguistic signposts by accurately indicating who says what to whom on what occasions and with what intent. But do the sociolinguistic facts need to be made explicit? Since people come to second language learning with complex social grammars from their own particular backgrounds, what items should be presented pertaining to the new language-culture? It is not as though L2 learners need to be instructed in 'politeness', but rather in those behaviors and linguistic forms of politeness which do not match their own. Because of this point, discussants have generally agreed that sociocultural aspects need to be cast quite differently from the traditional approach to grammar.

A further issue is the theory-to-practice question. Should writers look to the rules for speaking which exist to-date in the theoretical literature? According to one sociolinguist, 'The rules themselves may be well below the level of conscious awareness' (Wolfson 1983:63), adding that, 'While it is true that the intuitions of the native speaker may be a useful tool ... it is only through training in sociolinguistic analysis and through careful research that it is possible to discover the underlying patterns which make up the rules of speaking of any language, including one's own.' This recommendation implies that textbooks and materials concerned with sociocultural matter need to depend on the output of sociolinguistic research as their primary source.

However, the existing research may not be relevant for particular audiences. For example, of all the research topics in sociolinguistic investigations, terms of address probably has one of the longest listings in indexes and tables of contents. Should this topic, then, receive prominence in materials? Looking at the question from the theory-to-practice approach, the answer would probably be 'yes'.

A different view would start with an assessment of the learner-audience's needs, whether or not the theoretical literature could contribute insights on the particular sociolinguistic topics which the writers felt were necessary to include. Further, sensitive writers would undoubtedly take into account factors other than the needs of a particular audience: the actual context in which the topic is utilized, the demands of the marketplace for the topic in materials, etc.

Reliance on the output of linguistic research as the paramount source for language textbooks has yielded weak results in those cases where writers turned to grammatical analyses, devoting complete textbooks or large sections to topics currently in vogue: consider the proliferation of texts which presented the mechanism of sentence combining, or those that concentrated on the process of complementation. In many cases, the focus of such texts was too narrow for the needs of most programs.

Another lively issue for consideration is whether sociocultural aspects be presented to foster the goal of analysis or for productive use. Most likely the decision will depend on the particular circumstances in which the materials are to be used. Knowing about culture-dependent features of language may be valuable for people in literature courses in EFL settings, or the information may be significant for those who need a second language for purposes of travel. It is questionable, however, if in either of these cases course goals would be adopted which stress use or production of the TL since recognition would be adequate for these learners' needs. In turn, the determination of course objectives will help writers decide whether to concentrate on accuracy or fluency workouts. Where there is no set syllabus or curriculum, as is the case for textbook writers who work with the widest audience in mind, the decision becomes one which writers and editors alone make, basing their judgements on their perceptions of the marketplace.

For most writers, the decision to include sociocultural content in the materials will depend on criteria which are internal to the particular project. But no textbook which purports to represent how the language is actually used in communicative contexts can be produced without a sociolinguistic dimension. The choices which writers make regarding the characters, settings, and events all need to accurately reflect how L1 speakers use the language. With only a handful of models to follow, writers have an immense frontier to explore when they decide to deal realistically with the sociocultural component.

7.1.1   The state of the art

Following are examples of how teachers and writers have treated some of the issues. (See the *Practical Applications* section at the end of this chapter for additional comments on the following illustrated workouts in 1–7.)

I   MATCHING SITUATIONS AND UTTERANCES

(Janet Holmes and Dorothy F. Brown. 1976. 'Developing sociolinguistic competence in a second language'. *TESOL Quarterly* 10(4), pp. 421–3.) The example draws on students' own questions concerning appropriate language. Therefore, the writers assume that the situations involve an L2 learner as the speaker.

Illustration 7.1

EXERCISE: MATCHING SITUATIONS AND UTTERANCES

Part A. Match these situations with the responses that you think would be most appropriate. Remember that silence is sometimes an appropriate response.

Situation	*A Possible Response*
1. Getting out of a crowded bus.	How much is this, please?
2. Wanting to leave a party.	Excuse me, please.
3. Finding the cost of something.	Would you like some help?
4. Asking for tickets at the cinema.	I'm sorry, I'm a stranger myself.
5. Waiting at a bus stop with a stranger.	I think I'd better go now.
6. Seeing a friend for the first time since the death of his father.	Could you serve me, or are you busy?
7. Trying to get a shop assistant to serve you.	
8. Helping someone who has fallen over.	Two adults and one child upstairs, please.
9. Someone asks you the way but you are new to the town.	I was very sorry to hear that your father had died.
10. Seeing someone who is carrying many parcels.	Are you all right? Have you hurt yourself?

Part B. Now make up your own first remark for these situations.
(a) You have picked up a purse that you saw someone drop.
(b) Asking a friend to look after your child for two hours.
(c) Asking a shop to deliver a chair you have just bought.
(d) Telling a taxi-driver where you want to go.
(e) Giving your name to a clerk who can't spell it.
(f) Complaining about something you have bought which is not satisfactory.

Janet Holmes and Dorothy F. Brown. 'Developing sociolinguistic competence in a second languages'. *TESOL Quarterly* 10(4). Copyright © 1976 by Teachers of English to Speakers of Other Language. Reprinted by permission of the publisher and Janet Holmes and Dorothy F. Brown.

2   USING A STORY LINE

(Suzanne Griffin, 1981. *Follow me to San Francisco*, pp. 6–7. BBC English by Television.)
In this case, the situations draw on a video episode which, together with a student's text, comprise the instructional package. The workout puts the learner in the same situations that occur in the story line.

≫→

Illustration 7.2

J. Decide what to say

Each of the situations below is like one of the situations in the video episode. Choose the best expression to match the situation.

1. You are in a crowded bus. You bump into someone. You should apologize by saying:

   a. It's your fault.
   b. Oh, excuse me.
   c. Thank you.

2. You are offered something to eat. You don't want it. You should refuse politely by saying:

   a. How dreadful!
   b No, thank you.
   c. It looks delicious.

3. Someone is telling you a long story. You wish to show that you are listening. You should say:

   a. Really?
   b. I'm still listening to you.
   c. You're boring.

4. Someone has offered to help you, but you don't want help. You can refuse politely by saying:

   a. I don't need any help.
   b. Please leave me alone.
   c. Thanks for the offer, but I'd rather do this myself.

5. You want to ask a stranger a question. You should begin with:

   a. Certainly.
   b. Excuse me.
   c. Glad to meet you.

6. You want the operator to help you make a telephone call. You should begin your request with:

   a. Hey! Dial this number for me.
   b. Get me this number, will you?
   c. Hello, operator? I'm trying to call this number.

7. You have dialed the wrong number. When someone answers, you should apologize by saying:

   a. I'm sorry. I guess I dialed the wrong number.
   b. I'm sure I did it right.
   c. It's not my fault.

Suzanne Griffin, *Follow me to San Francisco*, pp. 6–7, © 1981, BBC English by Radio and Television.

3   SUGGESTING APPROPRIATE SITUATIONS

(A. Doff and J. Jones. 1980. *Feelings*, p. 15. Cambridge: Cambridge University Press.)
In workout A1, *Breathless moments*, the writers ask learners to supply

Illustration 7.3

Part two: Expressing the feeling

SECTION A: RECOGNITION

A1   Breathless moments

Look at the remarks below. Decide who the people are, what they're doing, and what they're excited about.

It's Spring, Arthur, Spring!

1 Ssh – look! A golden eagle! See the shape of the wings?
2 Come on, United! After 'em!
3 Yes, go on! Take his bishop! *That's* right!
4 Over there – on the horizon! Quick, get a fire going!
5 Ladies and Gentlemen. This is indeed a proud moment for me and, I trust, for all my supporters who turned out in such large numbers today. . .
6 See? 5.23 centimetres. Much too big for an ape.
7 Wait a minute. . .I know. It's. . .No, don't tell me. . .

A2   Postbag

Look at the following extracts from letters, in which the writers are looking forward to a meeting.

1 . . .I'm counting the days till the 17th. . .
2 . . .looking forward to seeing you on the 17th. . .
3 . . .see you on the 17th. . .
4 . . .I look forward to our meeting on 17 February. . .
5 . . .it'll be really great to actually meet you at last. . .
6 . . .it'll be good to get together again. . .

Which extract would you expect to see in a letter from:

a) a businessman you've never met
b) a businessman you often do business with
c) a penfriend
d) a close friend
e) an old friend who you haven't seen for a long time
f) someone who's in love with you

Which extracts express excitement most openly? Mark them on the scale below:

LEAST EXCITED: | | | | | | | :MOST EXCITED

the sociolinguistic variables: speakers, situations, and expressive tone. In A2, *Postbag*, learners match language expressions, as indicated in written register, with speakers.

Illustration 7.4

3.6 **That won't do**
(Dissatisfaction)

1 A: *But that's not green, it's turquoise!*
   B: *You didn't say what kind of green you wanted.*
   A: *Well . . . a . . . green green. I don't see what's so difficult about that.*
   B: *This was all I could get. It'll do, won't it?*
   A: *No, it won't. It doesn't go at all! Look . . .*

2 A: *And what's all this?*
   B: *That's the sky . . . and that's the grass.*
   A: *But that's no good. You've got them upside down.*
   B: *Why?*
   A: *Well, the sky's green and the grass is blue.*
   B: *Because I'm standing on my head.*

3 A: *This is the undercoat, is it?*
   B: *No, that's the finish. Microvinyl – doesn't need an undercoat.*
   A: *But where did you get that dreadful colour?*
   B: *You said you wanted the two greens mixed.*
   A: *I know . . . but this isn't what I had in mind at all. At all.*
   B: *Well, it's a bit late to start changing it now, in't it?*

4 A: *How do you like it?*
   B: *It's come out . . . very well, I think. I suppose you'll tone down the . . . green?*
   A: *No. Tone it down?*
   B: *Don't you find it a bit . . . gaudy?*
   A: *No. Not at all. Of course, if you don't like it . . .*
   B: *No, I do. No, really. It's . . . it's probably just the light . . .*

A. Maley and A. Duff, *Variations on a theme*, pp. 88–9, © 1978, Cambridge University Press.

4 INTERPRETING RELATIONS

(A. Maley and A. Duff. 1978. *Variations on a theme*, pp. 88–9. Cambridge: Cambridge University Press.)
The four short dialogues were written to illustrate degrees of politeness and status relationships between speakers. The authors leave it up to the learners to: (a) Rank the dialogues according to politeness. (b) Indicate the role relationships between speakers. (c) Indicate the situations and settings of each dialogue.

Interpretation

In which dialogues are the speakers most rude to each other? And most polite?
In which one do they know each other best?
What are the relationships between speakers in each dialogue? (i.e. friend to friend, husband to wife, customer to tradesman, etc.).
Where is each of the conversations taking place?
In dialogue 4, what does A really mean when he says, 'I suppose you'll tone down the ... green?'? And what does B really mean when he says, 'Of course, if you don't like it ...' in the same dialogue?
What is the green thing in each dialogue?

Some useful ways of expressing dissatisfaction

Awful/dreadful/disgraceful/hopeless/disgusting/rotten.
No good at all/not what we wanted/not up to scratch.
I'm not satisfied with/happy about ...
I can't say I liked/felt happy about/was satisfied with ...
It won't do/isn't good enough/is not satisfactory.
That's very bad.

Production

In pairs, discuss how one of the dialogues might continue if the person who is dissatisfied *insists* on a change in the colour. Write this out, then change partners and compare your different versions.

In our everyday lives, we are very often dissatisfied with the service we get or with the behaviour of others. Note down individually three examples from your own experience, then discuss these with the others in your group. What do you need to say to express your dissatisfaction?

5   SENSITIZING LEARNERS TO LANGUAGE VARIATION

(Brian Abbs and M. Sexton. 1978. *Challenges*, pp. 79, 81. London: Longman.)

Illustration 7.5

STEP 4 LISTENING + NOTE-TAKING

Listen to the short extracts of people talking. Try to decide WHO is talking to WHOM, WHERE and WHEN. Make notes under these headings:

Speaker	Hearer(s)	Place	Event

STEP 5 GROUPWORK: DISCUSSION

Discuss your notes with the other members of your group.

TASK 1

SITUATION GAME

In groups write a short extract of someone talking in English. It should not be too difficult to identify WHO is talking to WHOM, WHERE and WHEN. Record the extract and see if the other groups can work out WHO is talking to WHOM, WHERE and WHEN.

PROJECT 1

THE WAY PEOPLE SPEAK

You have now seen that:

People can use language to get across different intentions.

When you overhear people speak you can tell WHO is talking TO WHOM, WHERE and WHEN.

People speak English differently depending on which part of the country or which English-speaking country they come from.

They speak differently according to who they are talking to.

They speak differently according to where they are.

They speak differently according to what role they are playing.

TASKS

Think about somebody learning your language.

1. Make some recordings of people with different accents in your own language. Note down where they come from.

2. Take some of the speech intentions you have met in this unit. For each one, record and note down different ways of expressing it, according to who is talking, where the person is speaking and what role he/she is playing.

Finally, get together in groups and make up a combined phrasebook for your language under your speech intention headings.

Brian Abbs and M. Sexton, *Challenges*, pp. 79, 81, © 1978, Longman.

In these exercises, the authors present a series of workouts which sensitize learners to variation in language. First, there is a Situation Game (Task 1) which requires learners to produce 'a short extract' of spoken language. Next, learners hear a tape recording of seven speakers of English illustrating regional varieties: U.S., West Indies, India, Australia, Wales, North of England, and London (not shown here). Then, learners work on Project 1: 'The way people speak', tasks related to variation in their L1.

6   STATING A GENERALIZATION

(Ann Borkin and Susan M. Reinhart. 1978. 'Excuse me, I'm sorry'. *TESOL Quarterly* 12(1), pp. 57–69.)
This lesson presupposes that learners are confused with the two expressions, *excuse me* and *I'm sorry*. It shows examples of *excuse me* in the context of four dialogues, presents discussion questions about the examples, then presents a rule or generalization which points out how *excuse me* is used appropriately. In the last part of the lesson (not shown) there are situational roleplays which evoke spontaneous use of *excuse me* and *I'm sorry*.   »»→

Illustration 7.6

Excuse Me

PART I

Study the examples of *excuse me* in the dialogues below:

Dialogue 1

Situation: A man and a woman are sitting in a dentist's office. The woman takes out her cigarettes but can't find any matches.

Woman: Excuse me, do you have any matches?
Man: I think so. Just a minute. I'll look.

Dialogue 3

Situation: Mrs. Morgan is on a crowded bus and she needs to get off at the next stop. There is a man standing between her and the door.

Mrs. Morgan (to man): Excuse me.

Dialogue 2

Situation: Mike is having some friends over for dinner. They have just sat down to eat.

Karen: Mike, this soup is delicious.
       (telephone rings)
Mike: Excuse me. I'll be right back.

Dialogue 4

Situation: Frank and John are friends. They also work together in a shoe store. Right now Frank is helping a woman try on a pair of shoes. John comes to ask him a question.

Frank (to woman): We have that shoe in white and yellow.
John: Excuse me, Frank. Do you know the price of these sandals?
Frank: Those are $17.

Questions for Discussion

1. In Dialogue 1, how does the woman get the man's attention?
2. Why did Mike use *Excuse me* in Dialogue 2?
3. In Dialogue 3, what does Mrs. Morgan want to do? Why does she feel that she has to say something?
4. What is the reason John uses *Excuse me* in Dialogue 4?

Point to Remember

We use the expression *Excuse me* in English when we have broken a minor social rule, such as interrupting someone, trying to get someone's attention, asking someone to move, walking in front of someone, leaving a conversation before it is finished, etc.

Additional Note to Students: In English, *Excuse me* is sometimes used in formal situations, but not in informal ones. Here is one example:

Dialogue 5

Situation: John sees his friend Frank in the supermarket and calls to him.
John: Hey, Frank!
Frank: Hi, John. How's it going?

In an informal situation involving friends, *Hey, (name)* or *(Name)* are appropriate ways of getting someone's attention. In Dialogue 5, *Excuse me* would be considered too formal (and therefore not as friendly).

Why, then, in Dialogue 4, did Frank's friend John use *Excuse me* instead of *Hey, Frank*?

7 PRESENTING SITUATIONAL VARIATION CROSS-
  CULTURALLY

(Deena R. Levine and Mara B. Adelman. 1982. *Beyond language: inter-cultural communication for English as a second language pp. 29–30.* Englewood Cliffs: Prentice-Hall.)
In this illustration, the writers give a generalization about situational variation in language first, then they present the workout. The follow-up section at the end draws on learners' cross-cultural perceptions.

Illustration 7.7

Conversational Activities

A.   In English, as in other languages, the types of vocabulary, structure, and
Language tone used in conversation vary with the situation. Compare the ways
Style   that a request may be made; look at the vocabulary used and the length of
             the sentence in each of the following examples:

> I'm sorry to trouble you, but could you please tell me where the library is? *(formal)*
> Would you be so kind as to tell me where the library is? *(formal)*
> Where is the library, please? *(semiformal)*
> Where's the library? *(informal)*

Learning different styles in a second language is not always easy. It is necessary to know how to vary speech according to situations. Read the following situations and respond to each one appropriately.

1. There are discipline problems in one of your university classes. Students are talking all the time and you can't hear the professor or concentrate on the subject. You feel you must say something about the situation to your professor. You also want to tell a friend who is not in the class.

What would you say after class to your professor?

_____

_____

What would you say to the friend?

_____

_____

2. You need some money and you are considering asking either your parents or your friend for a loan.

How would you ask your parents?

_____

_____

How would you ask your friend?

_____

_____

3. You have just read an excellent article written by a student you know and a professor whom you don't know very well. You would like to compliment both of them on their well-written article.

What would you say to the student?

_____

_____

What would you say to the professor?

_____

_____

Follow-up: Look again at the above three situations and determine how you would respond in your *own* language. Are there formal and informal ways of expressing yourself? In your language, what words or grammatical constructions indicate formality and informality? Which situations call for formal speech and which call for informal speech?

Deena R. Levine, Mara B. Adelman, *Beyond Language*: Intercultural Communication for English as a Second Language, © 1982, pp. 29–30. Reprinted by permission of Prentice-Hall, Englewood Cliffs, New Jersey.

7.2 Scripting roleplays: a holistic view of sociocultural content

A ubiquitous workout of the communicative period, the roleplay turns up everywhere as a mode for comprehensive, holistic language practice. For writers, the roleplay is a high-gain, yet high-risk workout type since it has come to represent an array of assumptions about communicative goals in language pedagogy. Frequently used without any clear connection to a specific objective, roleplaying seems to imply that learners will acquire appropriate social norms of the target language-culture by assuming the identity of a member of that speech community. However, in most instances it is not at all clear just how the learners are supposed to get the information they need to adequately enact this identity.

But there is more to it, considering that in the language teaching profession, roleplay has become a cover term for a variety of types. Thus, writers tend to use names such as 'warm-up', 'improvisation', 'simulation', and 'socio-drama' somewhat willy-nilly as though there were little difference among them. Actually, the warm-up and improvisation have come into language teaching materials by way of the world of the theater (Spolin 1963). Simulations and socio-drama, no matter their exact origins, have been carefully delineated as classroom language teaching practices (Jones 1982; Scarcella 1978).

7.2.1 A brief geneology

Roleplaying, as it has been carried out in language teaching materials, has a distinguished but mixed heritage, tracing its antecedents to fields that include sociology, psychology, the theater, and education. The term *role* is a basic theoretical construct in sociology, lending itself to various classifications, mostly along a continuum which moves from basic to specific roles (Littlewood 1975). Thus, age or sex roles are regarded as basic; class or nationality are ascribed; social status or 'station in life' represent acquired roles; everyday transactions involving, for example, purchaser, seller, patient, etc., are actional roles; giving an order, expressing regret, or offering assistance are functional roles.

On the other hand, psychologists have made a distinction between social roles and 'the person who is playing the role' (Jourard 1964:23). So, roleplaying for psychologists has meant estrangement from self, or self-alienation. Jourard describes the condition this way: 'There is a Faustian drama in this world of roleplaying. Everywhere we see people who have sold their soul, or their real self, if you wish, in order to be a psychologist, a businessman, a nurse, a physician, a this or a that.' At the same time, some schools of psychotherapy have developed roleplaying as a therapy tool for getting a patient/client to 'know his self' (Jourard).

More directly related to language teaching is the cross-fertilization that has occurred during the past twenty-five years between practices in training actors for the theater and developments in education. Contemporary styles in acting call for spontaneity, authenticity, and naturalness. A primary source in this area is the work of Spolin (1963) who set out a highly structured sequence of dramatic exercises and activities – theater games – designed to prepare students of any age to act on the stage. The system had its origins in the author's work with children's games in Chicago settlement houses and reached its fullest artistic development in improvisational theater companies which took shape in the United States built on Spolin's theater games, reaching great popularity in the 1960s and 1970s.

Although Spolin apparently had no specific interest in the applications of her techniques to teaching in formal classroom settings, others saw the connections as notably evidenced in the work of Shaftel (1967) who developed roleplaying as a classroom technique for socializing young children in primary grades. She defined roleplaying as 'the spontaneous practice of roles – assuming them in order to practice the behavior required in various situations.'

When the goal of developing communicative competence in second language instruction became prominent in the 1970s, the language teaching profession also turned to roleplaying. Paulston (1977:32), for example, described roleplay as consisting of three basic parts: 'the situation, the roles, and useful expressions. Occasionally a section on background knowledge is needed for advanced roleplay.' But writers have not always followed this formula, as is illustrated in the next section.

7.2.2 *Issues for writers*

Can a little roleplaying be a dangerous thing? Most likely, if it is used indiscriminately. To avoid some of the pitfalls, writers are advised to:

I   AVOID PUTTING OLD WINE IN NEW BOTTLES

As indicated in illustrations 7.8 and 7.9, roleplay has been used as a title on many types of workouts, from old-fashioned dialogues to out-and-out interviews between partners. Putting a new label on an old, familiar workout type such as a dialogue is not an effective strategy by which to foster the goal of communicative competence. When there is no attention to the *role* and to the implications for the learner in assuming that role, then writers are better advised not to use the label.

Illustration 7.8

Description: *Places*

Role-playing dialogue

What are the roles? Not clear

Maggie is visiting a friend's flat.

MAGGIE: What a fantastic flat!
TESSA: *Do you like it?*
MAGGIE: Very much. I love the sitting room. It's got atmosphere.
TESSA: *Well you see Jack's a designer.*
MAGGIE: Is he?
TESSA: *Yes. He's an interior designer. He works for a firm of designers in London. He's got very good ideas.*
MAGGIE: And you've got some lovely paintings, haven't you?
TESSA: *My brother paints in his free time. They're his paintings.*
MAGGIE: But there are no chairs.
TESSA: *No, we haven't got a lot of furniture.*
MAGGIE: But where do you sit?
TESSA: *On the floor.*
MAGGIE: On the floor?
TESSA: *Yes, we sit on big Indian cushions on the floor.*

Brian Abbs, Angela Ayton and Ingrid Freebairn, *Strategies*, p. 20, © 1975, Longman.

Illustration 7.9

B Roleplay

Interview your partner. Find out about his job and background. Tell the rest of the class what you learn.

K. Morrow and K. Johnson, *Communicate 1*, p. 42, © 1979, Cambridge University Press.

2   PROVIDE A FOCUS

Every well-constructed language unit or lesson requires a focus, a point of concentration which the writer has selected. Next, the writer must consider: is roleplaying the optimum workout for this focus? If the role-play is in the materials for fluency practice, but without a content focus, then the writer needs to consider: 'Am I writing for actors-in-training or language learners?'

If a roleplay is intended to help learners understand social norms in the target language, then it must provide information about both the roles which learners are to assume and the social situations in which the roles are to be enacted. Illustration 7.10, for example, requires role-playing as an interviewer and a job applicant, although the authors do not make this fact clear. Also, it is not clear if the questions are 'embarrassing' to the interviewer or to the job applicant because we do not know enough about the situation. More than likely, the writers' attention was directed to the Hesitation Responders and Restatement Links. The material presents the possibility for roleplaying to take place, but in many classroom situations the fact might be lost sight of because the 'potentially embarrassing' questions and requests are given without enough information about the social roles and cultural values which are relevant in each case.

Illustration 7.10

G. RESTATEMENT

Well, uhm

Well, let's see

Well, let me think

*Let's put it this
way*

*I'll have to think
about that*

*RESTATEMENT
LINKS:*

**What you're saying
is**

**What you're really
saying is**

In other words

**You're simply
saying**

**If I understand you
correctly**

If I read you right

You mean then

**I know what you
mean**

TAKING SOMEONE ELSE OFF THE HOOK

Levels 2-4, pairs, speaking, 20 minutes

In this exercise, we re-enact an embarrassing situation many of us are familiar with:

INTERVIEWER: "How do you like your present job?"

*JOB APPLICANT: "Well, uhm, uh ... I don't really enjoy
all the in-fighting at work ..."*

*INTERVIEWER: "In other words, you don't really like some
aspects of your job."*

The interviewer accidentally (we hope) asked an embarrassing question, but when he realized that the job applicant had difficulties in answering, he took him off the hook with a forthright restatement of the answer. Now the burden of saying something unpleasant was on his shoulders, not the applicant's.

Break into pairs and go through such sequences using the suggested questions below, or with questions of your own.

POTENTIALLY EMBARRASSING QUESTIONS

1. *What is your religion?*
2. *You like golf, don't you?*
3. *Do you like cocktail parties?*
4. *You smoke a bit of grass (= marijuana) every once in a
   while, don't you?*
5. *I see on the application form that you are separated.*
6. *Your own embarrassing question*

POTENTIALLY EMBARRASSING REQUESTS

1. *Can you give me a letter of recommendation?*
2. *Can you give me some comment on this report?*
3. *Do you want to meet me for lunch?*
4. *Your own embarrassing request*

Eric Keller and S. T. Warner, 1976. *Gambits 2*, p. 22 (developed by the Public Service Commission of Canada). Reproduced by permission of the Minister of Supply and Services, Canada.

3 PROVIDE PREPARATION

Jumping into roleplaying without adequate preparation is a common failing in published materials. However, in illustration 7.11, the author provided a Note which helps learners and teachers workout more effectively.

Illustration 7.11

Improvisation

1. Your teacher will give you one of the situations below to improvise. Think about the situation, and discuss with your classmates what you would say and do.

2. With your classmates, show the rest of the class what you would say and do.

   Note: when you are preparing your improvisation, think about:
   the characters (how many? who?)
   the place (where? eg. an airplane flying across the Pacific)
   the time (when? eg. the present day, a weekday morning)
   the dialog (What will each person say?)
   the action (What will happen? What gestures and facial expressions will you use?)

Situation 1.
   You are on a long bus ride. You are very tired and you want to sleep. The nice lady sitting next to you wants to talk. After thirty minutes of conversation, you tell her that you must rest.

Situation 2.
   Your grandmother has made you a new dress (or shirt). She has worked very hard on it. She asks you to wear it to a family party. You don't like the dress (or shirt), but you thank her for the gift and you agree to wear it to the party.

Situation 3.
   You have arrived in a strange city. You plan to stay with a friend, but you don't know how to get to her/his place. You call your friend but there is no answer. You have your friend's address and you decide to go there on your own. You ask a stranger to help you.

Suzanne Griffin, *Follow me to San Francisco*, p. 6, © 1981, BBC English by Radio and Television.

4 DECIDE: PLAYING SELF OR OTHER?

An ambiguous point in language learning methodology concerns role-playing as either oneself or as someone else, presumably a target-culture member. On the one hand, the argument is made that the learner feels secure or safe wearing the mask, as it were, of another person. However, losing one's own identity is threatening (Piper 1983). Since a case can be made for both sides, the writer's task is not to solve the issue but rather to understand its ramifications by making clear-cut decisions in the writing of roleplays. Learners should either play themselves or others depending upon the focus and contextual features of the lesson at hand.

However, providing sufficient attention to both parts in a roleplay is also important. For example, in illustration 7.11, the writer has decided to have learners play themselves in situations which evolve from the story line in the materials. However, in this particular improvisation, the other person's role – in No. 1 the nice lady, in No. 2 the grandmother, and in No. 3 a stranger – is so bare of role designations that learners may not be able to play it successfully.

5 PROVIDE MOTIVATION

Having opted for playing the role of another, then the writer must build in strong motivational factors so that the learner wants to be that other person. Language learners, after all, are not actors-in-training. For example, in illustration 7.12 it is difficult to understand why learners would have interest in the roleplay since there is little that engages them actively in a story line. What appears to be missing is any kind of negotiation of outcomes (Candlin and Breen 1979), a factor which contributes vitally to motivation. Without a strong plot, or element of tension, the roleplay is without real reality (Taylor 1982).

[I quite agree with Dubin and Olshtain that this is a dull roleplay. It appeared in 1975 in what I expect was the first U.S. publication of roleplays for ESL, and we had yet to learn a lot about roleplay. Actually, 'The Research Paper' is not a roleplay at all but rather a rehearsal, and it worked in the classroom (all the exercises in the text were classroom tested) exactly because the students knew they were going to the library the following day. The motivation was external to the exercise, and as we know now, a roleplay must have some kind of problem to resolve if it is to come off. We have learned a lot about communicative activities in the last ten years and I hope we learn as much in the next ten.   Christina Bratt Paulston.]

≫→

Illustration 7.12

THE RESEARCH PAPER

Situation
You have been assigned a paper on a specific topic. It will be necessary for you to go to the library to look up material in both reference books and periodicals. The person at the ground-floor information desk will tell you that book listings are found in the card catalogue, and periodicals in the Readers' Guide. The periodicals are located on the fourth floor, and the books that you will need are on the third floor. The books may be checked out on the ground floor.

Role Assignments
  1. The Student Doing the Paper
  2. The Person at the Information Desk

Vocabulary
card catalogue	reference book
periodical	reference desk
journal	date due
ID card	stacks

The locations for the various library items listed above are particular to one library. The teacher should feel free to change any of the locations noted above in the "situation." The teacher may change these so that the role play can apply to any situation, or any location.

The lexical items listed above are important in doing library work, but the list is not exhaustive. The teacher should feel free to add vocabulary items which will aid the student in doing research work in the library.

Christina B. Paulston, et al. 1975. *Roleplays in English as a second language*, p. 4. Pittsburgh: University Center for International Studies.

In illustration 7.13 the writers have made the decision that learners will play the role of 'others', in this case Mr and Mrs Brown, adult members of the TL culture. The writers might consider: how can we build in elements in the workout which will provide the spark for motivation no matter what the ages or the backgrounds of the learners might be? Although there are conversations on tape between Mr and Mrs Brown, and information on their conflicting views in the textbook, in the way the workout appears, the burden is left to the teacher/director to enhance their characters and their motivations, particularly if the learners do not share the Browns' cultural background. In fact, learners from other cultures might well misunderstand the basis for the Browns' conversation. Of course, for learners who share the Browns' middle-class values regarding parenting, the underlying motivation for the roleplay would be comprehensible.

Illustration 7.13

3.1 Dialogue 🔈

It was such a long time since the Browns had heard from the Duponts in France . . . But one morning . . .
Listen . . .

3.2 A letter 🔈

> 15 avenue de Paris
> 76600 . Le Havre
> 15 April
>
> Dear John and Barbara,
>   I hope you still remember meeting us in London, six years ago at that accountants' conference.
>   I'm sorry that we haven't been able to meet again since. I still remember that small pub in Soho you took us to, and that long drive in the country in Surrey!
>   We haven't been able to repay any of this hospitality and I'm looking forward to this!
>   I remember you told us about your son Andrew; if I'm right, he must be 13 years old by now! You may remember we have a son, Eric, who is 15. Eric is studying English at school and his teacher said that a stay in England would do him good! I was just wondering whether you would be interested in sending Andrew to France? We could then organise an exchange. This is just a suggestion but could you let me know whether you are interested? We could then discuss details on the telephone.
>   We are looking forward to hearing from you.
>   Yours,
>   P. Dupont

3.3 Dialogue 🔈

Mr Brown is quite pleased with the letter, but his wife is more apprehensive.
Listen . . .

3.4 Mini role play

Work in pairs. One of you is Mrs Brown, the other Mr Brown.

Hicks, Poté, et al., *A case for English*, p. 14, © 1979, Cambridge University Press.

6   CONSIDER CROSS-CULTURAL IMPLICATIONS

In second language pedagogy, playing oneself, if it is to be authentic, usually means being a member of another culture. In illustration 7.14, the authors capitalize on the cross-cultural implications which evolve from roleplaying one's own cultural background.

Illustration 7.14

D.
Role-Plays
In pairs (if possible, with two people from the same culture*) write a dialogue *in your own language* and in English using the following situation. First perform the dialogue in front of the class in your own language. Then perform the same scene in English. The class members will comment on the nonverbal behavior they observe in both scenes.

> *Note: If class members are from one culture, role-play different situations (e.g., meeting a friend at a party, making a date, returning a bad product to a store manager).

D.
Role-Play
In small groups act out the following situations. Choose people to play each part and then decide which kind of introduction would be the most appropriate for each situation. Each member of the group should have an opportunity to make an introduction. Perform role-play in front of the rest of the class.

1. You are attending a school party and have brought your cousin to meet your teachers and friends. How would you introduce your cousin to the following people:

> Your classmate
> Your English teacher
> The director of the school

2. You are at a party with other students from the university. You don't know anybody and you'd like to meet a few people and start a conversation.

3. You are in the school cafeteria eating lunch when an American student sits down near you. Introduce yourself and initiate a conversation.

4. A friend of yours is introducing you to the Director of University Admissions. You want information about requirements. Initiate the conversation.

Follow-up: Discuss which introductions were the most difficult. In which situations did you feel the most comfortable?

7   PROVIDE A FOLLOW-UP

As important to motivation as are the elements that go into the roleplay itself is what comes afterwards. An opportunity to take stock of the workout could be a discussion, for example, around the question: 'Why did we do this?' In illustration 7.14, ('Follow-up' at the bottom of the page) learners discuss which introductions were the most difficult and in which did they feel the most comfortable. For roleplaying, the follow-up provides the generalization or rule-giving that is associated with the presentation of discrete elements in language. If learners are to come away with an understanding of the objective – the point of concentration – it must be included.

Practical applications

1. Using the seven illustrated workouts in section 7.1.1, do you think that each one stresses:
   (a) Goals of analysis or use?
   (b) Accuracy or fluency practice?
2. For writers, what are the benefits of establishing a story line, as in illustration 7.2, as the situational basis for workouts? In the workout, *Decide What to Say*, the writer addresses the learner. How might the writer present some sociolinguistic rules of variation tied to a shift in speaker by changing this direction?
3. In illustration 7.3, what must learners *already* know in order to do workout A1 *Breathless Moments*? A2 *Postbag*?
4. What learners (level, age, ESL/EFL, etc.) would benefit by the workouts illustrated in 7.4? What learners would be able to perform them? In the *Production* section, try to re-write the directions so that they are more explicit about the role relationships between the speakers.
5. What are the benefits and disadvantages of learners analyzing their own language for variation as shown in illustration 7.5?
6. What are the benefits and disadvantages of presenting a rule or generalization regarding the focus of the lesson? In illustration 7.6, the rule comes after learners have 'studied' the dialogues. Are there arguments for presenting it before the dialogues?
7. Compare the ways in which different writers bring in cross-cultural or contrastive sociolinguistic matters in illustrations 7.5 and 7.7. What are the strong and weak elements in each of the two examples?
8. Look back at the scales for assessing the cognitive and communicative potential of workouts in chapter 5, section 5.2. Using these scales as models, construct two additional scales that could be used to critique the workouts in a beginning level textbook: one scale for variety and one for student involvement or degree of participation.

References

Abbs, B., A. Ayton and I. Freebairn. 1975. *Strategies*. London: Longman.
Abbs, B. and M. Sexton. 1978. *Challenges*. London: Longman.
Borkin, A. and S. M. Reinhart. 1978. 'Excuse me, I'm sorry'. *TESOL Quarterly* 12(1), pp. 57–69.
Candlin, C. and M. Breen. 1979. 'Evaluating, adapting, and innovating language teaching materials'. In C. Yorio, K. Perkins and J. Schachter (Eds.). *On TESOL '79. The learner in focus*, pp. 86–108. Washington, D.C.: TESOL.
Doff, A. and J. Jones. 1980. *Feelings*. Cambridge: Cambridge University Press.
Griffin, S. 1981. *Follow me to San Francisco*. New York: Longman Inc. and London: BBC English by Radio and Television.
Hicks, D., M. Poté, A. Esnol and D. Wright. 1979. *A case for English*. Cambridge: Cambridge University Press.
Holmes, J. and D. F. Brown. 1976. 'Developing sociolinguistic competence in a second language'. *TESOL Quarterly* 10(4), pp. 421–3.
Jones, K. 1982. *Simulations in language teaching*. Cambridge: Cambridge University Press.
Jourard, S. M. 1964. *The transparent self*. Princeton: D. Van Nostrand Co., Inc.
Keller, E. and S. T. Warner. 1976. *Gambits 2*. Ottawa: Ministry of Supply and Services Canada.
Levine, D. R. and M. B. Adelman. 1982. *Beyond language: intercultural communication for English as a second language*. Englewood Cliffs: Prentice-Hall.
Littlewood, W. 1975. 'Role-performance and language-teaching'. IRAL XIII/3 (August), pp. 199–208.
Maley, A. and A. Duff. 1978. *Variations on a theme*. Cambridge: Cambridge University Press.
Morrow, K. and K. Johnson. 1979. *Communicate 1*. Cambridge: Cambridge University Press.
Paulston, C. B. 1977. 'Developing communicative competence: goals, procedures and techniques'. In J. Alatis and R. Crymes (Eds.) *The human factors in ESL*, pp. 20–39. Washington, D.C.: TESOL.
Paulston, C. B. et al. 1975. *Roleplays in English as a second language*. Pittsburgh: University Center for International Studies.
Piper, D. 1983. 'The notion of functional role-play'. *TEAL Occasional Papers* 7, pp. 20–39. TEAL association of British Columbia. Vancouver.
Scarcella, R. 1978. 'Sociodrama for social interaction'. *TESOL Quarterly* 12(1), pp. 41–6.
Shaftel, F. 1967. *Role playing for social values*. Englewood Cliffs: Prentice-Hall.
Spolin, V. 1963. *Improvisation for the theater: a handbook of teaching and directing techniques*. Evanston, Illinois: Northwestern University Press.
Taylor, B. 1982. 'In search of real reality'. *TESOL Quarterly* 16(1), pp. 29–42.
Wolfson, N. 1983. 'Rules of speaking'. In J. Richards and R. W. Schmidt (Eds.) *Language and communication*, pp. 61–87. Harlow: Longman.

8 Focusing on product: materials that deal with the reading skill

Overview

The preparation of reading materials for second-language instruction represents a striking example of the theory-to-practice model. Accordingly, in dealing with the skill of reading, the designer must synthesize various elements; thus, theory becomes embodied in the materials for instruction: (a) theories about the nature of reading itself, specifically models of mature reading; (b) the characteristics of reading selections, or textual analysis; and (c) the specific characteristics and needs of second language reader-learners. The purpose of this chapter is to show how this theory-to-practice model can be carried out.

In addition, this chapter by concentrating on materials for the teaching of the reading skill, makes clear our view that if the activity of materials writing is to be taken seriously, the 'how to' literature should be produced by those who have serious involvement with the particular area under discussion.

Beginning with *The materials preparer's role* in section 8.1, the discussion in chapter 8 then moves to an illustrated example of how a reading skills lesson was constructed in section 8.2. Section 8.3, *Guided questions for creating a reading lesson,* is a guided outline for writing a lesson which is derived from analyzing a particular text.

8.1 The materials preparer's role

Emphasis on setting objectives according to learners' purposes for studying second languages has brought about revived interest in the skill of reading, particularly in foreign language contexts where it takes on paramount importance. But unlike the static approach of earlier times when reading in a foreign language was usually done through grammar-translation, the communicative thrust has pushed forward the methodological discussion through attention to both learners' needs, textual properties, and recognition of the psychological and cognitive mechanisms associated with the complex skill of reading

8.1.1   The three elements

When concerned with skill in second and foreign language reading, the materials preparer functions as a mediator between the text and the learner-reader; this mediating process brings the learner in touch with strategies for successful reading which are utilized by efficient, mature native-readers. Thus, the materials designer's task is to synthesize three disparate elements into a compatible inter-relationship: (a) reading strategies, or a reconstruction of what an efficient native reader does – probably unconsciously, (b) textual analysis, or an examination of a text for the organizational and stylistic effects put there by the writer, and (c) second language learner-reader characteristics. The materials preparer tries to help the second language learner-reader actually experience what has been described for successful reading as 'a kind of accomplishment whereby a discourse is created in the mind by means of a process of reasoning.' (Widdowson 1978:63). The following paragraphs briefly summarize these three distinct constituents in the reading materials mix. Then, the role of the materials preparer is explored in further detail.

I.   SUCCESSFUL READING STRATEGIES

The designer draws on the considerable body of research into the reading process; most significant are reports on the nature of successful reading. To summarize tersely: good readers report using a wide variety of coping strategies – from the often mentioned skimming and scanning, guessing and predicting (Goodman 1979), to using internal and external context clues to derive meaning from texts. Prominent in any account of reading strategies is the ability of good readers to adjust to the material at hand (Gibson and Levin 1976), thus good readers quickly and possibly unconsciously fit their attack skills to their personal objectives for reading and to particular styles of writing. In preparing materials for the L2 learner-reader, the purpose is to recapitulate the ways in which mature readers get meaning from print by building in skill-giving workouts which concentrate on the process of reading itself. Attention to reading skills can range from the format in which the material is presented to actual workouts that are created for their appropriateness to the particular selection at hand.

2.   FEATURES OF THE TEXT

Textual analysis is concerned with the description of discourse, one aspect of which is work with written texts. This consists of analysis of how sentences and paragraphs are linked together to form larger texts, what Halliday and Hasan (1976) call 'texture'. Together with textual properties, there are structural features and cohesive relations; in English, for example, there are devices such as linking elements, reference and repetition. Then, too, there are organizational properties of texts, or what Widdowson (1978:45) has called 'coherence features', without which 'we cannot summarize, we can only quote.' Although the relations which hold elements in texts together are probably universal, the actual devices appear to be language specific.

The question of whether a good reader is consciously aware of textual features is an interesting, yet little explored area that richly deserves closer attention. We can only comment here that in our work with texts we often have not been consciously aware of discourse features in a particular text until after many readings of it, leading us to raise the question whether for second language reading it may be necessary to make conscious use of strategies for dealing with discourse which are only unconsciously sensed by the mature native reader.

In working with a wide variety of texts we have come to realize, too, that each one must be viewed individually, both in terms of its discourse features and in terms of learner-reader needs. So, for example, the designer, having scrutinized a promising text selection for its possible discourse components, then goes on to consider its usability with particular audiences, since all learner-readers, of course, do not have the same needs, interests, or background knowledge.

3. SECOND LANGUAGE LEARNER-READER
    CHARACTERISTICS

The materials preparer also takes into account differences in cultural background as well as difficulty with the new language. Along with discourse, attention to the syntactic and lexical characteristics of selections is vital. In fact, a number of problematic areas are continually being manipulated: (a) the linguistic competence of learner-readers; (b) the potential for cultural misunderstanding in the thematic content of the selections; (c) the element of personal background knowledge: do learner-readers have the necessary background or experience to understand the content of the selections? and (d) the degree of reading facility learner-readers possess in their native language.

8.1.2 The designer's task

An approach in which the materials preparer is concerned with strategies for effective reading, the nature of the reading passage, and learners' characteristics produces results which are different from those described in the last section. The materials preparer as synthesizer pays attention to the following:

I. WORKOUTS THAT BRING ABOUT INTERACTION WITH THE TEXT

The designer attends to the discoursal, syntactic, and lexical features in the text and reader interaction with the text. This goal is accomplished by developing types of workouts that facilitate interaction primarily with the reading selection at hand. A consequence of this approach is that a particular exercise type may only appear once in an entire textbook, while others may be more frequent. The preparers work out a general format, but the specific exercises are determined by the texts, not by a superimposed plan. This makes the learner's work, incidentally, less mechanical, and at the same time, more demanding.

2. PROVIDING A VARIETY OF MATERIALS TO READ

A good syllabus, course, or textbook should provide learner-readers with a variety of materials and with a variety of reading strategies. A current, covert attitude has been expressed in this statement: 'Such-and-such students only need to read English to be able to understand technical or scientific writing, so we will only instruct them in how to cope with one kind of material. They couldn't possibly want to read *Time, Newsweek* or *Playboy* since their purpose is reading-to-learn.' To this attitude, we say: The skill of reading is developed to maturity by reading what interests one and in reading as widely as possible. Good reading skills are developed by reading. For this reason, we prefer to design texts for intermediate and advanced levels which move students through various types of materials, from popular writing to textbook writing to professional writing – all quite different genres in English. All, by the way, are part of the type called expository writing.

3. SELECTING TEXTS APPROPRIATE FOR L2 LEARNER-READERS

Although current work in reading-to-learn has concentrated on more advanced learner-readers, there are vital needs at the other end of the continuum, learner-readers who are probably adequate readers in their first language but are at a low-intermediate or high-beginning level in language competence. In trying to match appropriate textual material with these abilities, we have found that for this level while expository writing selections are certainly appropriate, narratives are probably more productive.

There are a number of reasons for utilizing the narrative in a textbook for lower levels. First, narratives share universally the same kind of organizational feature, the element of chronology, making them an easier form for the inexperienced learner-reader. Second, the narrative seems to be a universal type of writing in all literate societies; learner-readers come to the rhetorical style of narratives with built-in experience. In addition, within the narrative type, there are many levels of complexity, affording the designer mechanisms with which to control and structure the selections. Four basic elements of complexity are determined by: (a) the degree of redundancy in the narrative, (b) the degree of given vs. withheld information in the plot, (c) the complexity of the characters, and (d) the complexity of the events.

By sequencing narratives according to their rating on these complexity scales, it is possible to provide lower level learners with experience in dealing with stated or implied information, main and supporting ideas, stylistic features used to elaborate main ideals, etc. (Dubin and Olshtain 1984). During the course, the materials preparers can gradually increase the degree of complexity of these four basic elements. For example, in a more advanced story the learner-reader needs to infer more information from the text rather than having everything spelled out. This kind of structuring of narrative elements makes it possible, too, to prepare learner-readers for doing critical reading or reading-between-the-lines at a later period.

Following the experience with narrative texts, the learner-reader can move on to unedited, expository texts intended for a large, popular audience. Here the purpose of reading is general information of a more factual nature. The analysis of such texts focuses on a variety of writing conventions which are typical of expository writing and which, contrary to the structure of the narrative, are more culture specific. The materials preparer incorporates reading strategies developed for narrative reading while adding new ones relevant to expository types, thus bridging the two.

The debate about whether to use original, simplified, abridged, or unedited so-called authentic texts has been raised frequently and from different views in the professional literature on second language reading. In the type of structured narratives we have described for low-inter-mediate reader-learners, it is necessary to turn to either originally written or carefully abridged narratives. As soon as possible, however, the use of authentic texts should become the objective, even if some adapting or abridging is necessary. In the following section, a complete reading lesson for an intermediate-advanced level is reproduced. This particular unedited text was selected, among other reasons, because it contains a narrative set within an expository framework, an excellent way to create a bridge into reading authentic texts.

8.2   A model reading lesson: 'A moral for any age' by Jacob Bronowski

The reading passage upon which the following comments are based appears on page 155.

8.2.1   *Strategies for developing reading skills*

The basic design of the unit incorporates a number of skill-getting devices for reading. Utilizing a modified version of the study skills formula SQ3R (Survey, question, read, review, recite) (Robinson 1961), the directions call for two readings of the passage. Preparation questions, or items to look for *During the First Reading*, cover main themes. Moreover, readers are encouraged not to use a dictionary during the first reading in order to activate the skill of skimming for the main ideas rather than relying on word-by-word reading. The questions *After the First Reading* are directed at the same main points. *During the Second Reading*, learners are guided into utilizing the organization of the writing as a means for understanding the supporting details.

Motivation is provided in the section *A Note About...* which contains background about the author and the passage. The information about a well-known TV program is included to evoke readers' possible prior experience with other materials written by the author. The photograph at the bottom of the first page is also included as visual preparation for the subject matter of the article. In case the keyword 'screwdriver' is not familiar in English, the photo provides pictorial meaning.

Following the workout section called *Applying Strategies*, the learners are given an opportunity to reinforce the ideas of the reading selection in *Talking About ...*, first through partner discussions, then in small groups. The section begins by asking questions directly related to the material, then they move to areas outside of the content of the selection, yet related to the readers' own lives and experiences.

8.2.2   *Features of the text*

The workouts in the sections *During the Second Reading* and *Applying Strategies* were written after a careful analysis of the textual elements in the passage. As the first lesson in a textbook which includes thirty-three such units, an effort was made to ease reader-learners into the style of the book. So, for example, in *During the Second Reading* an outline of the entire selection is given in order to emphasize the reading skill of taking in whole paragraphs at a time. Also, in F., *Finding Context Clues*, the idea behind contextual clues is introduced by gently cluing learners into finding the answers. Later context clue workouts will omit the intermediate steps that appear here.

Although the focus in C., *Locating Details*, is on verb tenses, the intent is not to include a traditional grammar exercise, but rather to help learners grasp how a shift in tense is used by this author to set off the segment in which a narrative unfolds.

As an example of the fact that exercises which draw on the textual characteristics of the passage itself are likely to turn up with rare types, workout E., *Looking for the Asides*, is the only one of its kind to be found among the thirty-three units, an occurrence which simply indicates that this particular stylistic device is not too widely used by authors – but it is used.

8.2.3 Accommodating learners' interests: working on hunches

Making decisions about reading selections to use with small, homogeneous groups of learners who are known to them can be a rewarding experience since in these cases the writers can put their efforts into finding passages which are tailor-made to the audience. However, textbook writers can only rely on their intuitions regarding topics of interest for large, heterogeneous groups.

Working on hunches, we decided to select *A Moral for Any Age* because of both its qualities of timeliness and timelessness. The topic of nuclear fission is the burning issue of the post World War II period. At the same time, the passage, since it tells of an event that already constitutes twentieth-century history, cannot become out-of-date.

But will the selection be of interest to intermediate-advanced learners of English in a variety of settings? The best effort that the materials writers can make is to take every social indicator into account, being careful to turn aside their own personal likes and dislikes as much as possible.

»»→

A MORAL FOR ANY AGE

A Note About ...

In this selection, Jacob Bronowski describes a real incident that took place in Los Alamos, New Mexico, the place where the first atomic weapon was developed. Professor Bronowski, who died in 1974, was a distinguished scientist, humanist, and optimist. He had faith in scientific thought and the human race. Professor Bronowski was the author of *The Ascent of Man* from which a famous television series was produced. "A Moral For Any Age" is an object lesson, a story that presents an example of right conduct. Through the telling of the story, Bronowski explains what morality means to him.

During the First Reading

Read the entire selection even if you do not know all of the words. Do not stop to look up unfamiliar words. Ask yourself these questions as you read:

- Which paragraph gives the background of the story?
- Which paragraphs give details about the story?
- Which paragraphs give Bronowski's purpose for telling the story?

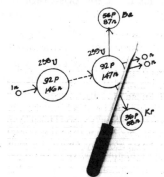

The formula for
nuclear fission.

A Moral For Any Age

JACOB BRONOWSKI

1 On May 12, 1946, Louis Alexander Slotin was carrying out an experiment in the laboratories at Los Alamos with seven other men. Slotin was good with his hands; he liked using his head; he was bright and a little daring—in short, he was like any other man anywhere who is happy in his work. At Los Alamos, Slotin, then aged thirty-five, was concerned with the assembly of pieces of plutonium, each of which alone is too small to be dangerous, and which will only sustain a chain reaction when they are put together. Atomic bombs are, in fact, detonated in this way, by suddenly bringing together several harmless pieces of plutonium so that they form a larger, explosive mass. Slotin himself had tested the assembly of the first experimental bomb which had been exploded in New Mexico in July, 1945.

2 Now, nearly a year later, Slotin was again doing an experiment of this kind. He was nudging toward one another, by tiny movements, several pieces of plutonium, in order to ensure that their total mass would be large enough to make a chain reaction; and he was doing it, as experts are tempted to do such things, with a screwdriver. The screwdriver slipped, the pieces of plutonium came a fraction too close together, and suddenly the instruments which everyone was watching registered a great upsurge of neutrons, which is the sign that a chain reaction has begun. The assembly was filling the room with radioactivity.

3 Slotin moved at once; he pulled the pieces of plutonium apart with his bare hands. This was virtually an act of suicide, for it exposed him to the largest dose of radioactivity. Then he calmly asked his seven co-workers to mark their precise positions at the time of the accident, in order that the degree of exposure of each one to the radioactivity could be fixed.

4 Having done this and alerted the medical service, Slotin apologized to his companions, and said what turned out to be exactly true: that he thought that he would die and that they would recover. Slotin had saved the lives of the seven men working with him by cutting to a minimum the time during which the assembly of plutonium was giving out neutrons and radioactive rays. He himself died of radiation sickness nine days later.

5 The setting for his act, the people involved, and the disaster are scientific: but this is not the reason why I tell Slotin's story. I tell it to show that morality—shall we call it heroism in this case?—has the same anatomy the world over. There are two things that make up morality. One is the sense that other people matter: the sense of common loyalty, of charity and tenderness, the sense of human love. The other is a clear judgment of what is at stake: a cold knowledge, without a trace of deception, of precisely what will happen to oneself and to others if one plays either the hero or the coward. This is the highest morality: to combine human love with an unflinching, a scientific judgment.

6 I tell the story of Louis Slotin for another reason also. He was an atomic physicist who made a different choice from mine. He was still working on bombs when he died, a year after World War II ended. I do not think the less of him because he took one view of a scientist's duty and I take another. For the essence of morality is not that we should all act alike. The essence of morality is that each of us should deeply search his own conscience—and should then act steadfastly as it tells him to do.

After the First Reading

What do you think is the main point of "A Moral For Any Age"? Select *one* from the list below:

- To warn people about the dangers of atomic power
- To describe the heroism of Louis Slotin
- To make a statement about what morality means

(Check your own answer after the Second Reading)

During the Second Reading

Now, read the selection a second time. Notice that it is organized into three sections: background information (paragraph one), the accident (paragraphs two, three, four), and the author's statement about morality (paragraphs five, six). While reading, look for the details in the three separate sections. Ask yourself these questions as you read:

Paragraph One: Background Information

- Who was Louis Slotin?

Paragraphs Two, Three, Four: The Accident

- What was he doing when the accident occurred?
- What caused the accident?
- How did he know the pieces of plutonium were too close together?
- Whose lives did he save?
- How did he save them?
- How accurately did he predict his own death?

Paragraphs Five, Six: The Author's Statement

- What two things, according to Bronowski, make up morality?
- What, according to Bronowski, is the essence of morality?

APPLYING STRATEGIES

A. Looking for Supporting Ideas

During the second reading, you used the outline of the main ideas. Now, look for the supporting ideas, the facts and details which build the main ideas. Circle any which are correct.

The Background

1. A description of Slotin
   a) Good with his hands
   b) Had tested first atomic bomb a year before
   c) Born in 1946

2. The assembly of plutonium
   a) One piece alone is harmless
   b) Several pieces brought together form an explosive mass
   c) Plutonium pieces are harmless

The Accident

3. Slotin's experiment
   a) A new type of experiment
   b) Similar to one done a year before
   c) Moving pieces of plutonium together

4. The incident that caused the accident
   a) Pieces came a fraction too close
   b) Experts never make mistakes
   c) Was using a screwdriver; it slipped

5. Slotin's act of heroism
   a) Pulled pieces apart with his hands
   b) Exposed himself to highest dose of radioactivity
   c) Asked co-workers to move from their positions

6. The result of his action
   a) Saved lives of seven men
   b) Died of radioactivity
   c) Did not predict his own death

The Author's Statement

7. Morality has two parts
   a) Other people matter
   b) One must have clear judgment
   c) The highest morality: human love together with scientific judgment

8. Bronowski's view of a scientist's duty
   a) We should all act alike
   b) We should each act according to our conscience
   c) Bronowski also chose to work on atomic bombs

B. Discovering the Thread of the Story

Writers weave their words together as craftsmen do a rug or tapestry. One way to provide unity in writing is by repeating an idea or element. Look at these phrases.

line 2: . . . good with his hands . . .

line 16: . . . the screwdriver slipped (from his hand) . . .

line 21: . . . his bare hands . . .

What is the thread (the repeated element) that ties together these phrases?

C. Locating Details

Look at these sentences from paragraph one. In them, the author gives supporting details about plutonium. These facts are not the main point of the paragraph so they are set off by using a different tense. The events of the story are in past tense; the supporting details in present tense.

Fill in the blanks with verbs in the form in which they appear in the first paragraph:

1. Louis Alexander Slotin _____ _____ out an experiment.

2. Slotin _____ _____ with the assembly of plutonium.

3. Each piece _____ too small to be dangerous.

4. They will only _____ a chain reaction when they _____ put together.

5. Atomic bombs _____ _____ by _____ together several harmless pieces of plutonium.

6. The pieces _____ a larger, explosive mass.

7. Slotin himself _____ _____ the first experimental bomb which _____ _____ _____ in New Mexico.

8. What tense is used in sentence 7 above? _____

9. Why is it used? _____

10. What tense is used in sentences 3, 4, 5, and 6 above? _____

11. Why is it used? _____

12. What tense is used in sentence 1 above? _____

13. Why is it used? _____

D. Finding the Time Signals

Look at these sentences. In them, the author links what happened a year before the accident with what happened at the time of the accident. Fill in the blanks with the words and elements which signal time.

1. Slotin _____ test ____ the first experimental bomb which _____ _____ explod ____ in New Mexico in 1945. _____ , nearly _____ _____ _____ , Slotin _____ _____ do _____ an experiment of this kind. He _____ nudg ____ several pieces of plutonium together. The screwdriver slipp ____ .

2. List the verb phrases in the paragraph above by tense form:
   past perfect:
   a) ____ _____
   past simple:
   b) _____
   past progressive (-*ing* form):
   c) _____

E. Looking for the Asides

Sometimes writers put in sentences that are not part of the narrative. These comments, called *asides*, are similar to what happens when an actor on the stage speaks directly to the audience. The punctuation tells you that the phrase or sentence is an aside. It contains information that comments on the main idea of the paragraph.

1. In paragraph two: Find the aside in lines 15-16. Write it on the line below. Make sure to copy the correct punctuation marks.

   _____

2. Choose one answer:
   In this aside, Bronowski is commenting on:
   a) Slotin
   b) Himself
   c) Experts

3. In paragraph five: Find the aside in line 34. Write it on the line below. Make sure to copy the correct punctuation marks.

   _____

4. Choose one answer:
   In this aside, Bronowski is commenting on:
   a) The disaster
   b) Morality
   c) Slotin's story

⟫→

F. Finding Context Clues

Frequently you can understand the meaning of new words by looking for clues in the same sentence or in the same paragraph. (A clue guides or directs you to the answer.) The words that help you understand unknown words are called "context clues." Guess the meaning of the *italicized* words at the left. The first example is done for you. In later exercises in this book, you will find the context clues yourself.

New words and expressions

1. Line 13: With tiny movements of his hands, Slotin *nudged* the pieces of plutonium toward one another.

2. Line 16: The screwdriver *slipped* out of his hand.

3. Line 18: The instruments registered an *upsurge* of neutrons when pieces of plutonium came too close together.

Context clues

1. *Clue:* With tiny movements of his hands = to move carefully, slowly

   So, *nudge* = to move carefully, slowly

2. *Clue:* out of his hand = to drop

   So, *slipped* = _____

   _____

3. *Clue:* up = think of upthrust, upward, upper

   So, *upsurge* = _____

   _____

Talking About . . .

Work with a partner and discuss these questions. Listen and respond to your partner's replies.

1. What were Slotin's alternatives when the accident happened?
2. What would you have done in Slotin's position?
3. Have you ever made a very quick decision that affected others' lives?

With your partner, join another pair to form a small group. In your small group, talk about these issues:

1. Do you believe the story about Slotin illustrates heroism, morality or both? Why?
2. Do you agree with Bronowski's definition of morality?
3. Do you know what a conscientious objector is? If not, look up the expression in the dictionary. Do you believe Bronowski approved of conscientious objectors? Have you had any experience with conscientious objectors? Share your ideas with the others in your group.

(from *Reading by all means* by Fraida Dubin and Elite Olshtain, © 1981, Addison-Wesley Publishing Co.)

8.3 Guided questions for creating a reading lesson

The questions below, intended for materials preparers who want to be able to use authentic texts for reading instruction, point out features which can be incorporated into exercises. The sections 8.3.1 and 8.3.3 concentrate on reading skill elements, while 8.3.2 is concerned with features in the text itself. The reading passage *Neutron Weapons:* upon which the steps are based, appears below and on pages 162–3.

Illustration 8.1

Neutron Weapons:

By J. GARROTT ALLEN

1   To minimize the horrendous devastation of nuclear warfare, exemplified by the bombing of Hiroshima and Nagasaki, the Reagan Administration has decided to produce the neutron warhead, which is designed to release enormous amounts of radiation while inflicting minimal damage to buildings and property in the targeted area. The principal advantage, we are told, is that the radiation would penetrate enemy tanks and rapidly kill military personnel, as well as anyone else within a radius of about 500 yards. There seems to be little awareness that many other people will receive lethal doses of radiation but will not die for weeks, months or even years. This poses medical problems of a magnitude never before considered.

2   Most physicians have not encountered patients heavily exposed to a sudden burst of ionizing radiation in which blast and heat are not components. I am one of the few who have.

3   During World War II, I was a physician on the Manhattan Project to build the first atomic bomb, and I witnessed the death of a 32-year-old physicist, Dr. Louis Slotin, who had been exposed to radiation during an accident at Los Alamos Scientific Laboratories in May, 1946. He was the leader of a group of eight men trying to join two pieces of nuclear material in order to create a critical mass. Slippage occurred that allowed a super-critical mass to develop momentarily, setting off an uncontrolled chain reaction and creating a sudden burst of ionizing radiation. Slotin had the presence of mind to immediately command the other seven persons

≫→

in the room to remain stationary until he could draw circles around their shoes. He did this in order to identify their location so that later on their clinical courses could be correlated with the dosage of rems (roentgen equivalent, man — a unit of radiation) that each received.

4   In less than an hour, all were admitted to the local hospital; in that brief time, Slotin had turned a tragic accident into the nearest thing that we have to a controlled human experiment on acute total body exposure to ionizing radiation. Slotin had already made a rough estimate of his own probable exposure dose as being more than 1,500 rems, and on that basis concluded that there was no hope for his survival. From numerous previous experiments on dogs exposed to ionizing radiation, there was no doubt that, if his calculations were correct, so was his prognosis.

5   His clinical course resembled that of some of the radiation victims in the Hiroshima and Nagasaki bombings 10 months earlier who had been in locations where heat and blast did not reach them. Much of this radiation was secondary, not direct, and resembled X-rays. Therefore, the exposure doses could not be nearly so well estimated. In the case of most of the fatalities, death was instantaneous from the heat and the blast, which extended beyond the bomb's radius of radiation.

6   The clinical results in Slotin's case duplicated what would happen to a person exposed to a nuclear tactical weapon, uncomplicated by the effects of blast and heat. During the first 12 hours, Slotin vomited several times and had diarrhea and a diminished output of urine. His hands, which had been the most heavily exposed to radiation, became swollen. Edema (swelling) and cyanosis (bluish discoloration) of the fingernail beds were noticed within three hours of the accident. Also, patches of erythema (redness) appeared on his hands and forearms. In 24 hours, erythema was also noted on the chest and abdomen. By the following morning, massive blisters had formed on his hands and forearms.

7   After the first day, Slotin developed adynamic ileus (paralysis of intestinal activity), which could be relieved only by the use of a continuous suction tube through the nose. This tube soon became painfully irritating because of ulcerations that developed on his tongue and in the back of his mouth and nose. His hands and

arms became increasingly swollen and painful. He required morphine for relief.

8   By the fifth day, diarrhea was frequent and uncontrollable. His hands had become gangrenous because the swelling had shut off the blood supply. The erythema and edema increased daily over his entire body. Frequent doses of morphine were the only treatment that was symptomatically effective. Nothing could be done to stop the steady progress of total disintegration of body functions.

9   On the ninth day, Louis Slotin died.

10   The autopsy findings were the same as those we had seen many times in experimental animals—hemorrhage throughout the body, the absence of platelets, and blood that would not clot.

11   The total body irradiation that this victim had received was later estimated at 1,930 rems. The other seven scientists in the room experienced much lower doses. The man standing immediately behind Slotin at the time of the accident, Dr. Alvin Graves, 34, received the second heaviest exposure, 390 rems. He eventually returned to work, directing many of the studies at the Nevada test site for several years before developing cataracts, becoming blind and dying at age 54 of other complications attributed by medical authorities in part to his radiation exposure in 1946. Two other members of Slotin's team subsequently died of acute leukemia.

12   There will be many survivors, both military and civilian, if and when nuclear tactical weapons are used. They will have received enough radiation to kill them, but for many death may be slow in coming. There is no effective medical treatment for serious radiation injury, and these deaths will be almost as agonizing to those looking on as to the victims themselves. The production of neutron weapons is probably as immoral a concept as human minds have yet devised.

J. Garrott Allen is a professor emeritus of surgery at Stanford University Medical School. He is a founding member of the Radiation Research Society and the author of numerous articles on the effects of radiation injury.

Los Angeles Times, November 11, 1981

8.3.1   Motivation for reading

This passage contains a narrative about the same historical incident that Jacob Bronowski wrote about in *A Moral for Any Age*. Thus, learners reading it following the Bronowski selection would already possess background knowledge about the subject matter, a vital element in reading comprehension.

1. How would you activate readers' previous knowledge of the subject matter to create motivation for reading this selection?
2. How would you acquaint readers with the author and his qualifications?
3. What other steps would you take as preparation for reading?
4. Is the title complete? Could this fact be utilized as motivation, or would you use it later in the lesson either as an issue for discussion or in a writing assignment?
5. What are important key words in the passage – words that appear frequently, sometimes in paraphrases, that are central to the main idea? How would you present these key words in order to aid reading comprehension?

8.3.2   Textual discovery procedures

As a vital aid for comprehension, skillful readers make use of organizational and stylistic elements, although they are probably unconscious of these textual features while reading. However, second and foreign language readers need to be guided into conscious awareness of how a text has been constructed – as an aid to reading. Effective reading materials provide exercises which help learners find features such as main and supporting ideas, words that link sentences and paragraphs along with other characteristics of the writing itself. The steps below are designed to lead you into discovering the organizational elements in the article on pp. 161–3 (*Neutron Weapons*): they are *not* intended as questions for L2 learners.

Read the article several times, looking for its organizational features. Try to find the paragraphs that contain main and supporting ideas. Where does the narrative occur? Then, use your findings to answer the following questions:

1. What action by the Reagan administration is mentioned? Is the author in favor of this decision?
2. Paragraph 2: Why is the author's experience unique?
3. Paragraphs 3–11: These paragraphs are all part of a narrative that is within the larger article. They tell the story of Dr. Louis Slotin. Which of these paragraphs (3–11) begin with expressions of time?

paragraph no.	time expression
....	....

....

....

4. Paragraph 6: Find three time expressions that link together the sentences

of paragraph 6: ...., ...,

....

5. Is paragraph 12 .... a summary? .... part of the narrative?
Suggestion: Look carefully at the verbs in paragraph 12 to find the answer.
6. The author's main reason for writing the article is stated in paragraph 12.
Find the sentence which best summarizes his overall point of view. Write
it in the space below:

....

8.3.3 Sharing ideas

Even though mature reading is an individual activity, motivation for
reading can be heightened through opportunities for talking about stimu-
lating ideas.
1. How would you guide an audience into further activities based on
their reading of the selection?
2. What further reading assignment might follow after this one?

8.3.4 Producing a reading lesson

Use your answers to the questions in sections 8.3.1, 8.3.2, and 8.3.3
to write an original reading lesson for L2 students in which you utilize
the text, *Neutron Weapons*. As a starting point for carrying out this
assignment, you may want to look back at the model reading lesson
A Moral for Any Age, or at some published reading skills textbook.

Practical applications

1. Select two or three potential passages for reading lessons that relate
to each other in terms of subject content. Try to find selections that
represent different types stylistically. For example, selections from
newspapers, popular magazines, professional journals, textbooks,
news magazines, etc.
Be ready to justify your selections in terms of the reading interests
and abilities of a particular audience: age, level of language competence, ESL or EFL.

2. Using one of the passages you have selected, make a careful analysis of the text. What organizational features lend themselves for inclusion in a reading lesson workout? What textual features lend themselves? For example, elements that connect sentences or paragraphs, elements that create cohesion or unity in the text.

References

Dubin, F. and E. Olshtain. 1981. *Reading by all means*. Reading, Massachusetts: Addison-Wesley.

Dubin, F. and E. Olshtain. 1984. *Three easy pieces*. Reading, Massachusetts: Addison-Wesley.

Garrott, Allen J. 1981. 'Neutron Weapons:'. *Los Angeles Times*, November 11, 1981.

Gibson, E. J. and H. Levin. 1976. *The psychology of reading*. Cambridge, Massachusetts: The M.I.T. Press.

Goodman, K. 1979. *Reading in the bilingual classroom: literacy and biliteracy*. Rosslyn, Virginia: National Clearinghouse for Bilingual Education.

Halliday, M. A. K. and R. Hasan. 1976. *Cohesion in English*. London: Longman.

Robinson, F. P. 1961. *Effective study* (revised edition). New York: Harper and Brothers.

Widdowson, H. G. 1978. *Teaching language as communication*. Oxford: Oxford University Press.

Other suggested readings

Dubin, F., D. Eskey, W. Grabe (Eds.) 1986. *Teaching second language reading for academic purposes*. Reading, Massachusetts: Addison-Wesley.

Grellet, F. 1981. *Developing reading skills*. Cambridge: Cambridge University Press.

Widdowson, H. G. 1979. 'The process and purpose of reading'. In *Explorations in applied linguistics*. Oxford: Oxford University Press.

9 Creating materials: the link between syllabus and audience

Overview

Creating materials through which people can effectively learn new languages is a highly specialized craft, one that seems to be perfected through immersion in the activity itself. Since the prospect of sink or swim can discourage potential talent, more attention needs to be paid to developing guidelines for writers. This chapter looks at writing in various ways: in section 9.1 *The audience for materials*, by contrasting writing for local or wider audiences, a difference often but not always marked by the separate worlds of producing non-commercial materials as opposed to commercial textbooks. In section 9.2, we differentiate between projects which are 'commissioned' and 'self-initiated'. In both, however, there is *Writing as a team effort*, the issue discussed in section 9.3. Finally, section 9.4 *A checklist for writers* is preparation for launching a materials writing project, or what to consider at the first meeting of a writing team.

9.1 The audience for materials

In an idealized model, materials draw on the content of a syllabus, reducing broader objectives to more manageable ones. In practice, however, course designs, although they may be available, possibly are not used by or are unknown to the teachers – most likely they are unknown to the learners. Indeed, the tangible element that gives a language course face validity to many learners and teachers is the textbook. The teacher's smudged handouts seldom carry the same air of authority (Dubin 1978). Although it is convenient to lump both together by calling them 'materials', in fact there are significant differences concerning the circumstances under which teacher-prepared materials and commercially sponsored textbooks come to be written, produced, and distributed.

To a certain extent, writing for a local or a wider audience coincides with the difference between non-commercial and commercially-sponsored projects. Of course this is not surprising inasmuch as educational publishers frequently though not in all instances look for materials that suit the widest possible audience, no matter what they consist of: audio, video, or computer software to fit the hardware; hands-on materials such as charts, wallboards, workbooks, paste-ons, etc.; along with all the other types that have two conventional covers. For writers, however, it is more productive to focus on the audience. That is why the terms 'local' and 'wider' are valuable.

There are times when a commercial firm might be asked to produce materials for a local audience, for a particular school, a particular system, a ministry, or even for an entire country. Then the commercial establishment actually produces materials for non-commercial purposes. But these cases are probably rare. Usually, non-commercial materials are aimed at a more specified, local audience. Commercial materials are for as wide an audience as possible.

9.1.1 Writing for a local audience

When they create for a local audience, the writers should be familiar with the needs of the learners, their age, level of proficiency, degree of motivation, cultural learning styles, etc. At the same time, there is usually complete information available about the instructional setting: class size, number of hours of instruction, place of the course in the curriculum, language(s) used by learners in and outside of the classroom, etc.

In this type of situation, too, there are probably well-defined goals. It is the job of the materials developers to write in harmony with the existing curriculum; also, coordination between the syllabus designers' and the writers' efforts is crucial. In fact, the writers probably know what school-leaving or national examinations are given, so they can produce textbooks which focus on specific skills and understandings. Such familiarization provides writers with a tremendous advantage, one which often supplies the original impetus for the materials writing project. However, knowing the audience well does not mean that writers can overlook, at an early stage, defining the scope of the project in terms of combining or emphasizing language skills, language content, and the processes in which skills and content are used.

Further, when writing for a well-defined, local audience, there is likely to be information about the teachers, their preparation, proficiency, and experience. If teachers are known to be non-fluent, writers try to design the textbook so that every step is set out; teachers only have to follow the recipe. Although this high degree of control is appropriate for beginning teachers, the disadvantage of such materials is that they cut down on initiative and creativity leaving little for teachers to contribute despite their command of the target language. Sometimes, after a year or two of working with tightly controlled materials, the teachers feel too bound. For this reason, writers who deal with a local audience often find they must walk a tightrope.

There are other problematic aspects as well with local audiences. Granted, the writers can select situations knowing whether or not learners possess the required background knowledge to understand them. However, cultural content presents some dilemmas. For example, supposing a team of writers is preparing a textbook for EFL learners, a local project in which the audience lives in non-urban settings. Suppose the situation selected for the unit is shopping. Should they present the learners with a typical American supermarket, using American labels, brands, and types of goods that one can buy in a supermarket in the United States? Should they use a picture of a supermarket with the kind of customer/clerk interaction that takes place there, or should they instead select a situation that is familiar to these learners? Which one is the more appropriate cultural context? True, the English language is used authentically in American supermarkets. But for these learners who may never get to see an American supermarket, is it real to speak in English in a grocery store?

There is an additional problem: while learning the target language content for a shopping situation, can the EFL learner also cope with new cultural elements? The situation suggests that grading or sequencing is necessary. The writers can start with the kind of grocery store that is familiar and still create a make-believe world where they assume, for the lesson, that English is spoken. Eventually, they can make the cultural themes more authentic in the second, third, and fourth year of the program. When they finally put an American supermarket into the lesson, they must be extremely accurate and generous in giving details. At this point, local writers need to check their work with native speakers for accuracy about the differences in cultural elements.

9.1.2 Writing for a wider audience

Many writers begin by creating for a local audience, or at least by using their experience with a known group of learners and a known instructional setting and then project these needs and specifications onto a wider framework. As with the inevitable distortion that takes place in enlarging any activity, something personalized may become lost in the process of translating localized needs onto a wide-focused screen. In fact, in most projects where the objective is to create for the widest possible audience – as in commercially sponsored undertakings – writers must grapple with the dilemma that one size never does fit all. This lack of fit of much that is written for a widest-possible-audience is a factor which persuades many local institutions to at least think about producing their own materials, given the resources of time and talent.

Although in writing for a wider audience it is much more difficult to take learners' characteristics into account, one difference that cannot be ignored is age. Children are not the same as adult learners. A more subtle age division is the one between children and adolescents. Where does the break occur? In producing for a wider audience, writers must also be aware that children in some cultures seem to mature socially more rapidly than in others. The writers often face a dilemma; they are either talking down to adolescents by using situations and contextualizations that are childish, or they are pushing their expectations for children beyond this audience's level of understanding.

But the most important factor in writing for a wider audience is not knowing the curriculum or syllabus, let alone the objectives of the audience. At times even educational goals are ill defined. In such cases, the writers themselves sometimes become the curriculum designers when their textbook is adopted, as was pointed out in chapter 2, section 2.3. Where there is an existing curriculum, it becomes the teacher's job to adjust the textbook written for a wide audience to local needs. However, writers must provide places in the text for these local adjustments to be made. One way is by giving enough practice material so that teachers are free to select what fits a particular group. But in many locales, users feel they should be able to finish a book in X number of hours. If all the lessons are not consumed in 60 or 90 hours, somehow the text has failed them. So, writers must continually maintain a balance – enough practice material to provide choice, but not so much that no one can finish the book.

9.1.3 Issues common to both audiences

Other issues of taste, sensitivity and attention to details are common to writing for both audiences, local and wide. For example, writers for either a local or wide audience might select two names like 'Joan' and 'John'. But how easily does the EFL or ESL learner recognize the difference between them since in terms of both sounds and spelling they are very similar? In terms of sounds, there are not many languages in the world which make a phonemic (meaningful) contrast between the sounds /o/ and /a/. Yet in English, the difference represents a contrast between a female and a male given name. To the eye, in terms of spelling, the two names look very much the same since they both begin and end with the same letter. One tends to overlook issues like these in choosing the elements that go into materials writing. Yet, the difficulties presented by small, culturally bound elements in language are quite crucial in writing for both audiences.

9.2 Commissioned and self-initiated projects

The source of motivation may not be evident when the effort is finally completed, but in terms of how the work is accomplished and what the internal demands on the writers are, the initiating impetus for a project is of great significance. Basically, writing projects are either commissioned by others or they are self-initiated by the writers themselves.

9.2.1 Commissioned projects

The trade-off in working on a commissioned project is that on the one hand the writers do not need to be concerned with finding a publisher to produce their efforts, on the other hand they probably have less opportunity to develop their own ideas. In such cases a governmental agency, an educational institution, or a publisher – perhaps some combination of the three – has commissioned the work. Because the audience and the thrust of the project has been established for them, the writers' tasks are likely to be more circumscribed.

The publisher or initiating authority may have set up a quality control person who follows the project from beginning to end, giving progress reports while the work is going on. The quality control person, most likely called an editor, is the project's coordinator, acting as liaison between writers and the commissioning authority. The writers, in turn, may simply be handed assignments having a small role in any of the brainstorming that puts shape to the overall objectives which the initiating agencies set forth. Thus, the writers feel that they never get far enough out of the forest to see the trees.

It may turn out, too, that a writing team for a commissioned project is made up of people from various backgrounds who have never worked together before. Their immediate assignment may be to produce together a sample unit or lessons within a short span of time. Jumping in without a sufficient period of either learning to work together efficiently or examining the full ramifications of the project itself may result in many problems being swept under the rug.

9.2.2 Self-initiated projects

When writers conceive their own projects there may be more personal satisfaction of various kinds; however, every step along the way, from the first bright idea to actual successful completion entails knowing the marketplace for materials very thoroughly.

Self-initiated projects usually start when an individual or a few teachers who have been successful in producing materials for their own immediate classroom needs decide that their 'great idea' deserves to be shared with

171

the rest of the world. However, some projects, whatever their intrinsic worth, never get beyond this stage primarily because the writers do not stop to think seriously about the differences between materials for class-room use and the requirements for a publishable textbook. It is certainly true that a worthwhile textbook requires insights from teaching, but it also requires craftsmanship from writers.

What is frequently necessary is for the teachers/writers to put aside their successful classroom materials and to think about the specialized requirements of a textbook. Although classroom materials can fill many file drawers since they are chronologically-based, a textbook is finite in terms of the number of pages it contains; it is spatially-based (Dubin 1978). A good book really begins with an agreed-upon size and shape. It may turn out, too, that the teachers'/writers' good ideas do not have applicability beyond the local audience with whom they have been used. Or, the needs of their particular audience may be too narrow, thus the materials need to be severely reworked.

A key factor in transforming either classroom materials into a publish-able manuscript or transposing one's own 'great idea' into a book depends on having a grasp of the marketplace for textbooks. Getting a book to a prospective publisher at the right time in terms of trends and developments in the field is as important as the publisher getting it into the marketplace at the right time. Being either too early – when there is not yet interest in the idea – or too late – simply following in many others' footsteps – is poor timing.

It is often up to the writers to assess the field; the publisher, with all good intentions, is not in a position to keep up with trends in language teaching along with a number of other subject areas in his/her educational catalog. In such a case, the writers must be able to supply a prospective publisher with enough background information to support their propo-sal. That is why having the widest possible understanding of both ESL and EFL teaching situations is vital. Basing a proposal in terms of one's own classroom experience is a good beginning but is not sufficient.

One way to keep abreast of what is being published in the ELT field is by looking carefully at the wares displayed by publishers at teachers' conferences and conventions. Putting one's name on publishers' mailing lists for copies of announcements of new offerings and catalogs is also helpful. By getting to know the types of educational materials and texts which particular publishers produce, an author with aspirations to be published can make better decisions regarding which editors or pub-lishers to approach with sample ideas and lessons.

9.2.3   'I have an idea . . .'

'I have an idea. What do I do now?' The customary reply to that question is as follows: Prepare a table of contents, a brief descriptive statement (called either a rationale or a prospectus), at least two sample lessons, units or chapters, and send it off to the publisher who seems to be aiming at the audience you have in mind for your own work. It helps considerably to have had some face-to-face contact with the editor–publisher, or their representative, to whom you send your work. If you don't receive an acknowledgement that your package has been received by them within a couple of weeks after sending it, follow up with a polite inquiry.

'I don't know what to put into the rationale. What should it include?' Essentially, (a) describe the scope of the project and its objectives; (b) describe the teacher/learner audience for whom you are writing (age, language level, educational background, etc.); (c) give a statement about any significant organizational features, possibly highlighting the table of contents; (d) provide a brief summary of other published or unpublished texts similar to your own (the competition); (e) briefly sketch the authors' qualifications. Make it short and readable. Try to personalize it to the particular editor–publisher to whom it is addressed.

'What will the publisher do with the material I send?' In most cases, your sample lessons and rationale will be sent to reviewers for appraisal, a process that can stretch over a few months at least. In other words, the publisher will rely heavily on the comments which seasoned professionals (who usually receive a small fee from the publisher for their service) report back. These reviewers' comments may well contain useful suggestions that will guide you in further shaping of the work.

9.3   Writing as a team effort

Because of the variety of tasks which must be performed, together with the advisability of bringing in various skills, talents, and points of view, writing is frequently a team effort or a co-authored venture.

This team effort characteristic of materials writing projects brings 'who' questions into focus: Who takes responsibility for organizing the work? Who controls quality? Who watches the clock – and the budget? Who speaks for the teacher's role? Who for learners' needs? Who negotiates with editors/publishers when the writing is for a wider audience? Who deals with administrators, ministers, or deputies when the product is being prepared for a more local audience?

9.3.1   An idealized team

No matter the number of people involved, a joint or team effort brings out idealized personality types and special talents. Of course, in a co-authorship one member usually personifies various roles and possesses multiple areas of expertise. As in any partnership that works well, each person needs to enhance the other. Fundamentally, the basic element is trust.

It goes without saying that all members of a materials writing team will have professional qualifications for the assignment. But in putting together a team, consideration should be given to each member's area of specialization: A good team should have a balance of interests with at least one grammatical expert along with people who have strong backgrounds in language learning theory and sociolinguistics. At the same time, when it comes to organizing the writing, members' particular talents need to be heeded. Some will work more effectively as originators or conceptualizers, some will be effective finishers, while others would be best assigned as polishers or re-write specialists. In an effective team at least, members complement each other. A successful materials producing team is composed of personalities who have learned to compensate for individual weaknesses by using each other's strengths. In fact, a strong team needs divergent personality types so that there is ample opportunity for a flow of ideas.

For example, a team needs an organizer, someone who tactfully lays out the tasks which need to be accomplished. The team needs an idea person, the one who has flair and imagination. At the same time, the team requires someone who is a hard worker, the diligent person who sticks to the job no matter what the interference is. Then, too, there is bound to be a worrier, a defeatest type who, by injecting an air of negativism into meetings, helps the others view the optimist's remarks in the cold light of reality.

A good team should have an experimenter, as well as an evaluator. Those who have worked with teams report that inevitably there is 'a big talker' as well as a persuader, the one who can argue strongly for a particular decision. Along with all of the types listed, the team must also have a finalizer, the one who reminds the others to keep on the track so that the job will finally be completed.

Effective committees as well as teams operate through democratic processes. But anyone who has worked on a committee knows there must be one person at the head. Someone must be selected to make the final decisions. That individual needs to be sensitive to others yet wise enough to know how and when to maneuver so that everyone's abilities are utilized.

9.3.2   Other team models

There is also team writing which follows an authoritarian format. One person, totally responsible for conceptualization and design, assigns the tasks. Since the work is highly structured, it is apt to be completed more punctually. However, as in any rote operation, there is an absence of creativeness. The products of this kind of team effort are usually easy to pick out because of the mechanical, production-line stamp on the pages. All units, all exercises are likely to be exactly the same as though a mold had been cast and those contributing have poured in filler material.

9.4 A checklist for writers

The decision-making characteristic of materials writing is most apparent during the early stages of a project. To avoid unnecessary re-writing at later periods, many basic problems should be settled early. The questions below can serve as a checklist when the work is just beginning to take shape. Resolving all of them may actually stretch over a longer period than just one meeting, but by carefully defining the project during the early stages, later problems can be anticipated or possibly avoided. In fact, through a discussion of basic issues in the early meetings, members have an opportunity to learn more about each other's characteristics as team participants, affording any who find group decision-making too restricting an opportunity to reconsider the commitment. Similarly, the head of the team can use the experience of the first meeting to plan assignments based on actual working experience with each of the members.

9.4.1 Questions about basic assumptions

1. Conceptualization: Is the projection really worth undertaking or are we re-inventing the wheel? Are there existing materials or texts that will serve the purpose?
2. Definition: Are we trying to incorporate the universe or only a manageable part of it?
3. Objectives: Have we clearly assessed actual needs and goals of our intended audience? How will these needs and goals be realized in our project?
4. Congruence: Have we related the project's objectives to those of any syllabus or curriculum that was produced to guide us? If we are not working with an established syllabus, how will we go about making decisions regarding what language content to include: grammatical structures, situations, themes or topics, functions, and lexis.
5. Voice: Whose voice will speak from the pages, the writers', in the guise of the book, or the teacher's? If it is the writers' voice, how will we make it clear when the voice speaks to the teacher, to the learners, or when it represents the teacher to the learners? Should we address learners and teachers in separate texts?

6. Teachers: Who will retain the most control, the teacher in the classroom or the materials writers through the pages of the text? How much authority will the teacher be given? Will procedures be explicitly or loosely set out, giving the teacher room to expand and improvise?

7. Learners: How much responsibility will they be given? What contribution will they make to the learning process? Will they work individually, in pairs, in groups, or as a whole class through frontal teaching as in a teacher-centered classroom? Are the modes of learning selected compatible with their cultural expectations about what materials should provide? How will we account for differences in learning styles in our audience?

8. Neutralism or particularism: Will there be an identifiable point of view embedded in the language content in terms of age, sex, social class, nationality, educational status, lifestyle, etc.?

9. Inventiveness: How will we provide internal structure to lessons or units without boring our audience because of repetitive processes?

10. Skills: How will we integrate the language skills we have chosen to emphasize with language structures, themes, situations, or functions?

9.4.2   Questions about shape and design

1. Length and size: What dimensions are we working with? If our project is to be publishable, we must determine an approximate length. If we are writing materials for local use, we must consider how to use our resources for maximum effectiveness.

2. Internal format: What will constitute a lesson? A unit? A section? Will each contain the same elements? Will we rely on one workout type or should we provide variety? Will we have uniform titles on sections, lessons, workouts, etc.?

3. Sequencing/grading: In what order will the separate parts be presented? Should the lessons increase in difficulty? Should we consider a matrix, a story line, or cyclical ordering?

4. Processes: What will teacher/learners do before the lesson (preparation)? What will they do during the lesson (workouts) and afterwards (reinforcement)? How will we provide learners with occasions for utilizing elements of the lesson outside of the classroom?

5. Consumable: Should we design pages so that learners use them up, for example, by writing in them? If we are thinking about a publishable text, this approach may have advantages, but for local materials quite the opposite criteria might be important.

6. External format: How will we title the materials? Package them? Mount them? What graphic devices can we utilize to enhance their appeal?

7. Ancillary: What additional elements should be included? For example, for publishable: word lists, glossary, index; for local materials: picture file, art work, realia.
8. Visual and auditory aids: Should we incorporate additional visual or auditory components? For example, use of video, film, radio, taperecording, etc.?
9. Options: How can we provide alternative choices in the materials to ensure that teachers and learners have the means for adapting the work more readily to their own needs?
10. Evaluation: What measures will we include for assessing learners' mastery of the content? How will we field-test work in progress?

Practical applications

1 Work in small groups:
Create a fictional cast of characters based on the list below. Begin by establishing a specific setting in which these characters live and work (it could be mythical, of course). Then, give each of the characters specific characteristics regarding at least the following: age (approximate), sex, professional experience, personality traits, status designation, educational viewpoint, language-culture background, personal biases.
   - a representative of an educational publishing company
   - a representative of a governmental bureau or agency
   - a group of ELT writers/teachers (they have been selected to work as a team)
   - an educational administrator to whom the writing team reports
   - a trend-setter in the field who serves as a consultant
2 Make up a situation which casts the characters you have created in an interactive scene that calls for resolving a point of controversy. Begin by establishing the issue. Then, think about these questions: Who are the advocates? Who supports whom? Who are hold-outs? Who are rebels? Who are sell-outs? The controversy might involve issues such as these:
a) The funding source for the project, a government agency, through its representative reports at the first meeting that it will be necessary to cut back the original scope of the project by 50%. However, another publishing company (not represented at the meeting) has informally agreed to match the government funds if it receives full publishing rights, thus easing out the publisher who was initially involved with the team. The government representative seems to be in favor of this plan, although he is reluctant to press the issue. However, some of the writers are personally connected with the publishing company which is represented on the team.

b) The trend-setter who has been asked to serve as a consultant is, in fact, already committed to another publishing company as an editor for a project which is somewhat related in subject and scope but will be carried out in another country. Some members of the team feel that the trend-setter should resign because of conflict of interests. They are waging a cloak-room campaign to force the trend-setter to resign from the team. However, the trend-setter has some strong supporters among the writers.

3 Share your ideas for a developed simulation which includes a cast of characters and a mini-plot with the other groups, then listen to their simulations. Select one simulation to carry out in full-blown fashion by assigning roles and coming to a consensus regarding the controversy.

4 Either draw on your own experience or on your imagination to briefly outline a hypothetical materials writing project. You should specify facts concerning the following:
   a) Audience: Learners: age, level, ESL/EFL
                  Teachers: educational backgrounds, target language
                             proficiency, native language backgrounds
   b) Type of instructional setting:
                  higher education, vocational ...
   c) Motivation for the project:
                  lack of existing materials, offer of grant money ...
   d) Other contingencies:
                  You create them.

5 Use the hypothetical project which receives the highest number of votes by the group for simulating a first meeting of a materials writing project, including a minimum of three people but no more than seven. Use the checklist for writers in section 9.4 as the agenda for the first meeting. Before starting the group meeting, select a chairperson, a notetaker and a timekeeper.

6 After the first meeting of the materials writing team, assess your own strengths and weaknesses as a team member. Ask yourself: 'Am I a productive member of a writing group, balancing my conflicting tendencies towards cooperation and competitiveness? Do I work at my best when decision making is carried out in a situation in which group dynamics is paramount?'

References

Dubin, F. 1978. 'The shape they are in now and the shape of textbooks to come'. In C. Blatchford and J. Schachter (Eds.) *On TESOL '78. EFL policies, programs, practices*, pp. 128–36. Washington, D.C.: TESOL.

Other suggested readings

Low, G. 1979. 'Teaching materials design'. *The English Bulletin* VII(2): 40–50.
Methold, K. 1972. 'The practical aspects of instructional materials preparation'. *RELC Journal* 3 (No. 1 & 2), pp. 88–97.

Epilogue

In covering new ground and by looking at the field in a different manner, we are aware that many issues have been raised in these pages which require further expansion and development. However, if nothing else, we hope that *Course Design* kindles interest in the relatively unexplored areas of course planning and materials writing for ESL/EFL. Indeed, we also realize that by dealing with both these topics in one book – actually, in following the steps suggested by Taba (see Introduction) – we have staked out a very large piece of turf, so much so that many of the issues which have come up have received far from exhaustive treatment. However, we have chosen this wide scope because, as language teaching professionals who design courses and write materials, we know only too well how limited the literature in these areas is.

Particularly concerning materials writing, we have had to contain our coverage within quite selective topics: one chapter which concentrated on a particular aspect of language content – sociocultural appropriateness – (chapter 7); one which concentrated on a single skill – reading – (chapter 8); and a last one which presented an overview of professional concerns about the writing craft itself (chapter 9). In other words, the field is still wide-open.

Certainly we have not intended to promote a particular 'method' or 'approach'. *Course Design* was not meant to further communicative language teaching in the way too many 'approaches' and 'methods' have been offered to language teaching specialists. But since it is the spirit of our times, we have adopted it to illustrate the framework for course designing which has been developed here.

At this point, it is worth saying something about course evaluation – the last phase in general curriculum building in Taba's model – which has so far been omitted in this book. A formidable world in itself, even taking a single step into it seems to open up multiple issues for discussion. But in any framework for building courses, the final step must be some form of evaluation of the work which has been produced by the designers. In the terms in which the issues have been developed here, evaluation should be directed to all levels in the framework: to the curriculum or statement of policy, to the syllabuses for separate courses, and to the materials that are produced for use by teachers and learners in connection with those courses.

Essentially, in assessing the result of the designers' work, two basic questions must be asked:
1. Has the curriculum/syllabus/set of materials produced the desired results?
2. How can the curriculum/syllabus/set of materials be improved?
However, the ways of assessing results and delineating means for improving instructional plans might be very different depending on the philosophical/theoretical basis of those plans themselves. Accordingly, assessment might be carried out in an informal manner, relying on subjective reactions of the participants – teachers, learners, and all others concerned with the program. On the other hand, assessment can be quite formal, drawing on the technical field of assessment and evaluation which exists for general curriculum instruction.

If an informal approach is adopted, the question that might be raised in some circles is: what validity do these findings have?

But if a formalistic set of evaluation measures is used, the important question for language course design is: what validity do those procedures have in terms of our knowledge of the nature of human language and the way in which language is acquired? Ultimately, formal assessment of the results of language programs cannot avoid getting into questions about testing students' language competence.

In turn, questions of language testing lead inevitably to the dilemma of discrete elements vs. holistic use of language, an issue which was discussed at some length in chapter 6. In fact, the field of language testing is plagued by this very problem. Clearly, however, delving into issues of language testing goes beyond our interests in this book.

However, course designers need to look for external measures that make use of holistic devices through which to evaluate the results of syllabuses and materials. For example, in an academic ESL course, an assessment of the success of the syllabus can be made by gathering information on how well students are achieving in their other subject matter courses. If ESL students' performance in terms of earned grades is comparable with native speaker students then the program is meeting an important goal. Or, if students take ESL classes before they are admitted to regular classes, long-range studies can be undertaken which track students' progress in terms of grades, length of time taken to earn diplomas, degrees, etc.

Similarly, in vocational purposes courses, studies of learners' success in holding a job in which they must use English, or adequate use of English for conversational purposes with co-workers and supervisors are both assessments of the outcome of the ESL program.

While formal assessment of all types may be appropriate in language programs which must meet criteria of 'accountability', in other cases the use of subjective evaluation measures may actually be more in harmony with the basic philosophy established in the statement of policy – the curriculum. If a program has been built upon humanistic educational goals which favor course outcomes such as helping learners to become better language learners, then subjective measures of evaluation may be to the point.

Subjective evaluation in humanistically inclined programs should be carried out by both teachers and learners. Although they would not necessarily answer the same questions, ideally they would share their views with each other. From the learner's point of view, evaluation questions might ask:

1. Has my attitude toward language learning changed in any way as a result of my experience in this course?
2. Am I more willing to try new modes of learning as a result of this class?
3. Am I more self-confident in using the target language both within and outside the classroom as a result of this class?

Along with asking themselves questions about their effectiveness in the role of directing other people to do things through using the target language, a teacher's subjective evaluation might also be in the form of a daily/weekly journal about what happened in class. By recording how one felt about the outcome of each session over a period of time, a teacher can compile a valuable data-bank for use by the designers in assessing the results of the instructional plans.

The subjective measures described so far depend on teachers and learners assessing their own behavior, not always an easy task. However, there are other ways to evaluate the results of humanistically-inclined programs by observing the success, degree of enthusiasm, and productivity evidenced by both teachers and learners in carrying out the workouts through which language practice has been specified in the syllabus.

The perspective presented in *Course Design* has been from the point of view of the designer who plans *for* learners. It seems to us that in the interest of developing specialists who can carry out course planning and materials writing assignments this outlook is necessary. Yet, we find that we cannot write about teachers and learners sharing in evaluation without, even in this final paragraph, adding the note that to be in accord with the philosophy of humanistic education, learners, too, must be brought into the activity of course planning by working with designers and teachers to establish goals and objectives which are in keeping with their particular needs. In this way, learners engage in designing their own plans for language learning.

References

Taba, H. 1962. *Curriculum development: theory and practice.* New York: Harcourt Brace and World.

Cumulative bibliography

Abbs, B., A. Ayton, and I. Freebairn. 1975. *Strategies*. London: Longman.

Abbs, B., and M. Sexton. 1978. *Challenges*. London: Longman.

Alexander, L. G. 1976. 'Where do we go from here? A reconsideration of some basic assumptions affecting course design'. *English Language Teaching* 30(2), pp. 89–103.

Allwright, R. L. 1972. 'Prescription and description in the training of language teachers'. In J. Qvistgaard, H. Schwarts, and H. Spang-Hanssen (Eds.) *Proceedings of the third International Congress of Applied Linguistics* (AILA: Copenhagen 1972), pp. 150–66. Heidelberg, Julius Groos Verlag.

Allwright, R. L. 1982. Talk before faculty and students, Master's program in Applied Linguistics, University of Southern California (March).

Alvin, M., and C. Kraft. 1982. 'Instructor's Handbook for Intermediate Academic English: 201'. American Language Institute, University of Southern California.

Anthony, E. M. 1963. 'Approach, method, and technique'. *English Language Teaching* 17 (January), pp. 63–7.

Bateson, G. 1955. 'A theory of play and fantasy'. In J. S. Bruner, A. Jolly, and K. Sylva (Eds.) *Play, its role in development and evolution*, pp. 28–64. 1976. Harmondsworth: Penguin Books.

Baudoin, E., D. Baber, M. Clarke, B. Dobsen, and S. Silberstein. 1977. *Reader's choice*. Ann Arbor: University of Michigan Press.

Bloom, B. S. (Ed.) 1956. *Taxonomy of educational objectives*. New York: David McKay Co. Inc.

Blum-Kulka, S., and E. Olshtain. 1984. 'Requests and apologies: a cross-cultural study of speech act realization patterns'. *Applied Linguistics* V(3), pp. 196–214.

Boey, Lim Kiat. 1979. 'Issues in the teaching of English as a second language in Malaysia'. In Feitelson.

Borkin, A., and S. M. Reinhart. 1978. 'Excuse me. I'm sorry'. *TESOL Quarterly* 12(1), pp. 57–69.

British Council. *English Teaching Profile 1979.*

Brumfit, C. J. 1979. ' "Communicative" language teaching: an educational perspective'. In C. J. Brumfit and K. Johnson (Eds.) *The communicative approach to language teaching*, pp. 183–91. Oxford: Oxford University Press.

Brumfit, C. J. 1981. 'Notional syllabuses revisited: a response'. *Applied Linguistics* II(1), pp. 90–3.

Bruner, J. 1972. 'Nature and uses of immaturity'. In J. S. Bruner, A. Jolly, and K. Sylva (Eds.) *Play, its role in development and evolution*, pp. 28–64. 1976. Harmondsworth: Penguin Books.

184

Canale, M., and M. Swain. 1980. 'Theoretical bases of communicative approaches to second language teaching and testing'. *Applied Linguistics* I(1), pp. 1–47

Candlin, C. and M. Breen. 1979. 'Evaluating, adapting, and innovating language teaching materials'. In C. Yorio, K. Perkins and J. Schachter (Eds.) *On TESOL '79. The learner in focus*, pp. 86–108. Washington, D.C.: TESOL.

Capra, F. 1982. *The turning point*. New York; Simon and Schuster.

Celce-Murcia, M. 1980. 'Language teaching methods from the ancient Greeks to Gattegno'. *Mextesol Journal* IV(4), pp. 2–13.

Chomsky, N. 1965. *Aspects of the theory of syntax*. Cambridge, Massachusetts: M. I. T. Press.

Cohen, A. D. and C. Hosenfeld, 1981. 'Some mentalistic data in second language research'. *Language Learning* 31(2), pp. 285–313.

Corder, S. Pit. 1977. 'Language teaching and learning: a social encounter'. In H. Brown, C. Yorio and R. Crymes (Eds.) *On TESOL '77. Teaching and learning English as a second language: trends in research and practice*. Washington, D.C.: TESOL.

Cummins, J. 1978. 'Bilingualism and the development of metalinguistic awareness'. *Journal of Cross-cultural Psychology* 9, pp. 131–49.

Cummins, J. 1979. 'Cognitive/academic language proficiency, linguistic interdependence, the optimal age question and some other matters'. *Working Papers in Bilingualism* 19, pp. 197–205.

Cummins, J. 1980. 'The contrast of language proficiency in bilingual education'. Paper presented at the Georgetown Round Table on Languages and Linguistics.

Cummins, J. 1981. *The role of primary language development in promoting educational success for language minority students. Schooling and language minority students: A theoretical framework*. Los Angeles: Evaluation, Dissemination, and Assessment Center, California State University, Los Angeles.

Curran, C. A. 1972. *Counseling-learning. A whole person model for education*. New York: Grune and Stratton.

Doff, A., and J. Jones. 1980. *Feelings*. Cambridge: Cambridge University Press.

Dubin, F. 1978. 'The shape they are in now and the shape of textbooks to come'. In C. Blatchford and J. Schachter (Eds.) *On TESOL '78. EFL policies, programs, practices*, pp. 128–36. Washington, D.C.: TESOL.

Dubin, F., and M. Margol. 1977. *It's time to talk*. Englewood Cliffs: Prentice-Hall.

Dubin, F., and E. Olshtain. 1981. *Reading by all means*. Reading, Massachusetts: Addison-Wesley.

Dubin, F., and E. Olshtain. 1984. *Three easy pieces*. Reading, Massachusetts: Addison-Wesley.

van Ek, J. A. 1977. *The threshold level for modern language learning in schools*. London: Longman.

Erikson, E. H. 1972. 'Play and actuality'. In J. S. Bruner, A. Jolly, and K. Sylva (Eds.) *Play, its role in development and evolution*, pp. 688–703. 1976. Harmondsworth: Penguin Books.

Eskey, D. E. 1983. 'Meanwhile back in the real world ... accuracy and fluency in second language teaching'. *TESOL Quarterly* 17(2), pp. 315–23.

Fanselow, J. F. 1977. 'Beyond Rashomon—conceptualizing and describing the teaching act'. *TESOL Quarterly* 11(1), pp. 17–39.

Feitelson, D. 1979. *Mother tongue or second language? On the teaching of reading in multilingual societies*. Newark, Delaware: Newbury House.

Fishman, J. A., R. L. Cooper and W. W. Conrad. 1977. *The spread of English: the sociology of English as an additional language*. Rowley, Massachusetts: Newbury House.

Gardner, R. D. and W. Lambert. 1972. *Attitudes and motivation in second language learning*. Rowley, Massachusetts: Newbury House.

Gattegno, C. 1972. *Teaching foreign languages in schools: The Silent Way*. New York: Education Solutions.

Gattegno, C. 1983. 'The Silent Way'. In J. Oller and R. Amata (Eds.) *Methods that work*. Rowley, Massachusetts: Newbury House.

Gibson, E. J. and H. Levin. 1976. *The psychology of reading*. Cambridge Massachusetts: M. I. T. Press.

Goodman, K. 1979. *Reading in the bilingual classroom: literacy and biliteracy*. Rosslyn, Virginia: National Clearinghouse for Bilingual Education.

Grellet, F. 1981. *Developing reading skills*. Cambridge: Cambridge University Press.

Griffin, S. 1981. *Follow me to San Francisco*. New York: Longman Inc. and London: B.B.C. English by Television.

Gumperz J. J. 1968. 'Types of linguistic communities'. In Gumperz 1971.

Gumperz, J. J. 1970. 'Verbal strategies in multilingual communication'. In J. E. Alatis (Ed.) *21st Annual Georgetown Round Table of Languages and Linguistics*, pp. 129–47.

Gumperz, J. J. 1971. *Language and social groups*. pp. 97–113. Stanford: Stanford University Press.

Halliday, M. A. K., and R. Hasan. 1976. *Cohesion in English*. London: Longman.

Harrison, W., C. H. Prator, and R. G. Tucker. 1975. *English language policy survey of Jordan: a case study in language planning*. Arlington, Virginia: Center for Applied Linguistics.

Holmes, J. and D. F. Brown. 1976. 'Developing sociolinguistic competence in a second language'. *TESOL Quarterly* 10(4), pp. 421–3.

Howatt, A. P. R. 1984. *A history of English language teaching*. Oxford: Oxford University Press.

Hymes, D. H. 1962. 'The ethnography of speaking'. In T. Gladwin and W. Sturtevant (Eds.) *Anthropology and human behavior*, pp. 13–53. Washington, D.C.: Anthropological Society of Washington.

Hymes, D. H. 1964. 'Toward ethnographies of communication'. In J. J. Gumperz and D. H. Hymes (Eds.) 'The ethnography of communication'. Special issue: *American Anthropologist* 66(6) part 2, pp. 1–34.

Hymes, D. H. 1972. 'On communicative competence'. In J. B. Pride and J. Holmes (Eds.) *Sociolinguistics*. Harmondsworth: Penguin Books.

Johnson, K. 1982. *Communicative syllabus design and methodology*. Oxford: Pergamon Press.

Jones, K. 1982. *Simulations in language teaching*. Cambridge: Cambridge University Press.

Jourard, S. M. 1964 *The treatment self*. Princeton: D. Van Nostrand Co., Inc.

Kaplan, R. 1966. 'Cultural thought patterns in intercultural education'. *Language Learning* 16, 1–2, pp. 1–20.

Kaplan, R. 1972. 'The anatomy of rhetoric'. In R. C. Lugton (Ed.) *English as a second language: current issues*. Philadelphia: Center for Curriculum Development.

Keller, E., and S. T. Warner, 1976. *Gambits 2*. Ottawa: Ministry of Supply and Services Canada.

Kelly, L. G. 1969. *25 centuries of language teaching*. Rowley, Massachusetts: Newbury House.

Krashen, S., and T. Terrell. 1983. *The natural approach: language acquisition in the classroom*. San Francisco: Alemany Press, and Oxford: Pergamon Press.

Labov, W. 1970. 'The study of language in its social context'. *Studium Generale*, 23, pp. 30–87.

Levine, D. R., and M. B. Adelman. 1982. *Beyond language: intercultural communication for English as a second language*. Englewood Cliffs: Prentice-Hall.

Littlewood, W. T. 1975. 'Role-performance and language-teaching'. IRAL XIII/3 (August), pp. 199–208.

Littlewood, W. T. 1981. Communicative language teaching. Cambridge: Cambridge University Press.

Los Angeles Unified School District 1982 revision. *Course outline for English as a second language, levels 1–4*. Los Angeles: Adult/Regional Occupational Centers/Program Education Division.

Low, G. 1979. 'Teaching materials design'. *The English Bulletin* VII(2), pp. 40–50.

Maley, A. 1983. 'I got religion! Evangelism in TEFL'. In M. Clarke and J. Handscombe (Eds.) *On TESOL '82: Pacific perspectives on language learning and teaching*. Washington, D.C.: TESOL.

Maley, A., and A. Duff. 1978. *Variations on a theme*. Cambridge: Cambridge University Press.

Maslow, A. 1954. *Motivation and personality*. New York: Harper.

McKay, S. 1980. 'Towards an integrated syllabus'. In K. Croft (Ed.) *Readings in English as a second language*, pp. 72–84. Cambridge, Massachusetts: Winthrop Publishers, Inc.

McLaughlin, B. 1981. 'Difference and similarities between first and second language learning'. In Winitz (Ed.) *Native language and foreign language acquisition*. New York: Annals of the New York Academy of Sciences, vol. 379.

McNeil, J. D. 1977. *Curriculum: a comprehensive introduction*. Boston, Massachusetts: Little, Brown and Company.

Methold, K. 1972. 'The practical aspects of instructional materials preparation'. *RELC Journal* 3 (No. 1 & 2), pp. 88–97.

Morrow, K. 1981. 'Principles of communicative methodology'. In K. Johnson and K. Morrow (Eds.) *Communication in the classroom*. Harlow: Longman.

Morrow, K. and K. Johnson. 1979. *Communicate 1*. Cambridge: Cambridge University Press.

Munby, J. 1978. *Communicative syllabus design*. Cambridge: Cambridge University Press.

O'Neill, R. 1970. *English in situations*. London: Oxford University Press.

Paulston, C. B. 1977. 'Developing communicative competence: goals, procedures and techniques'. In J. Alatis and R. Crymes (Eds.) *The human factors in ESL*, pp. 20–39. Washington, D.C.: TESOL.

Paulston, C. B. 1981. 'Notional syllabuses revisited: some comments'. *Applied Linguistics* II(1), pp. 93–6

Paulston, C. B. *et al.* 1975. Roleplays in English as a second language. Pittsburgh: University Center for International Studies.

Piper, D. 1983. 'The notion of functional role-play'. *TEAL Occasional Papers* 7. pp. 10–39. TEAL association of British Columbia, Vancouver.

Reich, C. A. 1970. *The greening of America*. New York: Random House.

Richards, J. C. 1984. 'The secret life of methods'. *TESOL Quarterly* 18(1).

Rivers, W. 1980. 'Foreign language acquisition: where the real problems lie'. *Applied Linguistics* I(1), pp. 48–59.

Rivers, W. 1981. *Teaching foreign-language skills*. Second edition. Chicago: Chicago University Press.

Rivers, W. and B. J. Melvin. 1981. 'Language learners as individuals: discovering their needs, wants and learning styles'. In Alatis, Altman and Alatis (Eds.) *The second language classroom: directions for the 1980s*, pp. 79–93. New York: Oxford University Press.

Robinson, F. P. 1961. *Effective study*. (revised edition) New York: Harper and Brothers.

Roget's Thesaurus (Ed. S. M. Lloyd) 1982. Harlow: Longman.

Rubin, J. 1975. 'What the good language learner can teach us'. *TESOL Quarterly* 9, pp. 41–51.

Sacks, H. 1972. 'An initial investigation of the usability of conversational data for doing sociology'. In D. Sudnow (Ed.) *Studies in social interaction*, pp. 31–74. New York: The Free Press.

Sanders, N. 1966. *Classroom questions: what kinds?* New York: Harper and Row.

Sapir, E. 1921. *Language, an introduction to the study of speech*. New York: Harcourt, Brace and World. (Harvest Books).

Scarcella, R. 1978. 'Sociodrama for social interaction'. *TESOL Quarterly* 12(1), pp. 41–6.

Schachter, J. 1981. 'A new account of language transfer'. Paper presented at Language Transfer Conference, Ann Arbor, Michigan.

Schegloff, E. A. 1968. 'Sequencing in conversational openings', *American Anthropologist* 70, pp. 1075–95.

Schumann, J. H. 1978. 'Social and psychological factors in second language acquisition'. In J. C. Richards (Ed.) 1978. *Understanding second and foreign language learning*. Rowley, Massachusetts: Newbury House.

Schumann, J. H. 1982. 'Art and science in second language acquisition research'. In M. Clark and J. Handscombe (Eds.) *On TESOL '82. Pacific perspectives on language learning and teaching*, pp. 107–24. Washington, D.C.: TESOL.

Searle, J. R. 1969. *Speech acts. An essay in the philosophy of language*. New York: Oxford University Press.

Seliger, H. W. 1983. 'Strategy and tactic in second language acquisition'. In K. M. Bailey (Ed.) *Proceedings of the third Los Angeles second language research forum*. Rowley Massachusetts: Newbury House.

Shaftel, F. 1967. *Role playing for social values*. Englewood Cliffs: Prentice-Hall.

Spolin, V. 1963. *Improvisation for the theater: a handbook of teaching and directing techniques*. Evanston, Illinois: Northwestern University Press.

Stevick, E. 1971. *Adapting and writing language lessons*. Washington, D.C. Foreign Service Institute. (Superintendent of Documents, U.S. Govt. Printing Office, 20402.)

Strevens, P. 1980. *Teaching English as an international language: from practice to principle*. Oxford: Pergamon Press.

Sutherland, K. (ed.) 1980. *English Alpha*. Boston, Massachusetts: Houghton Mifflin Company.

Swan, M. and C. Walter. 1984. *The Cambridge English Course, Student's Book 1*. Cambridge: Cambridge University Press.

Taba, H. 1962. *Curriculum development: theory and practice*. New York: Harcourt, Brace and World.

Taylor, B. 1982. 'In search of real reality'. *TESOL Quarterly* 16(1), pp. 29–42.

Titone, R. 1981. 'The holistic approach to second language education'. In Alatis, Altman, and Alatis (Eds.) *The second language classroom: directions for the 1980s*, pp. 67–77. New York: Oxford University Press.

Trim, J. L. M. 1984. Extract from 'Developing a unit/credit scheme of adult language learning'. In J. A. van Ek and J. L. M. Trim (Eds.) *Across the threshold*. Oxford: Pergamon Press.

Wallerstein, N. 1983. *Language and culture in conflict: problem posing in the ESL classroom*. Reading, Massachusetts: Addison-Wesley.

Wattinger, J. R. 1984. 'Communicative language teaching: a new metaphor'. *TESOL Quarterly* 18(3), pp. 391–407.

Widdowson, H. G. 1978a. 'Notional-functional syllabuses: 1978'. In C. Blatchford and J. Schachter (Eds.) *On TESOL '78: EFL policies, programs, practices*, pp. 33–5. Washington, D.C.: TESOL.

Widdowson, H. G. 1978b. *Teaching language as communication*. Oxford: Oxford University Press.

Widdowson, H. G. 1979. 'The process and purpose of reading'. In *Explorations in applied linguistics*. Oxford: Oxford University Press.

Wilkins, D. A. 1976. *Notional Syllabuses*. Oxford: Oxford University Press.

Wilkins, D. A. 1981. 'Notional syllabuses revisited: a further reply'. *Applied Linguistics* II(1), pp. 96–100.

Wolfson, N. 1983. 'Rules of speaking'. In J. Richards and . W. Schmidt (Eds.) *Language and communication*, pp. 61–87. Harlow: Longman.

Yalden, J. 1983. *The communicative syllabus: evolution, design, and implementation*. Oxford: Pergamon Press.

Acknowledgements

The authors and publishers are grateful to the following for permission to reproduce material:

Addison-Wesley Publishing Company: extract from *Reading by all means* on pp. 154–60. Dr. J. Garrott Allen: 'Neutron Weapons:' on pp. 161–3. Mary Alvin and Cheryl Kraft: extract from the American Language Institute, University of Southern California Instructor's Handbook for Intermediate Academic English: 201 on p. 53. B.B.C. English by Radio and Television: extracts from *Follow me to San Francisco* on pp. 63, 126 and 140. Cambridge University Press: extract from *The Cambridge English Course* 1 on pp. 112–13; extract from *Feelings* on p. 127; extract from *Variations on a theme* on p. 128; extract from *Communicate* 1 on p. 137; extract from *A case for English* on p. 143. Houghton Mifflin Company: extract from *English Alpha* on p. 52. Sadae Iwataki, Supervisor Adult ESL Programs: Preface to the Los Angeles Unified School District 1982 revision – course outline for ESL, levels 1–4 on p. 41. Longman Ltd.: extracts from *Strategies* on pp. 62 and 137; extract from *Challenges* on p. 130. The Minister of Supply and Services Canada: extract from *Gambits* 2 on p. 139. Oxford University Press: extract from *English in Situations* on pp. 56–7. Christina Bratt Paulston: extract from *Roleplays in English as a second language* on p. 142. Prentice-Hall: extract from *It's time to talk* on pp. 58–61; extracts from *Beyond language: intercultural communication for English as a second language* on pp. 134 and 144. TESOL and J. Holmes and D. F. Brown: extract from 'Developing sociolinguistic competence in a second language' on p. 125; TESOL and A. Borkin and S. M. Reinhart: 'Excuse me, I'm sorry.' on p. 132.

Index

accuracy and fluency, 73, 116
acquisition heuristics, 71
acquisition of language, 27, 32
approach to teaching, 64
assimilation – acculturation, 18
attitudes: affective domain, 48; assessment of, 15; individual and group, 13–17; negative, 14; positive, 14; questionnaire, 15–17; towards educational framework, 69; towards nature of language, 69; towards nature of learning, 69; towards target language, 13
affective (domain), 48
audience: local, 168–9; wider, 169–70
audiolingual view, 48

behaviouristic psychology, 74

checklist for writers, 175–7
classroom: setting, 31–2; size of, 32
cognitive: processes, 68, 71; potential of workouts, 99–100
cognitive-code approach, 35, 46
coherence features, 149
cohesive relations, 149
communication (communicative): ability, 28; channel, 69; competence, 93; curriculum, 68, 88; language teaching, 66, 68; misconceptions of, 88; needs, 38; processes, 94; view of language, 35
community: speech, 70
Community Language Learning (CLL), 64, 78
competence: communicative, 70; linguistic, 149

content, 45, 149; in communicative syllabus, 88–9; organization of, 46; situation, 58; sociocultural, 124; thematic, 45
context (social), 69
course formulation, 41
culture: (cross-) cultural implications, 78; (and) educational philosophy, 41; (and) language, 123; potential for misunderstanding, 149
curriculum see syllabus, 2, 3, 28, 40; absence of specific policy, 44; advisory committee, 24; audience, 23; audiolingual, 35, 46, 69; basis for designing, 23; committee, 24; communicative, 68, 88; competencies, 24; components of, 35–6; content of, 15–6, 49; decision making, 18; definition of, 34–5, 40; design, 18, 68, 69, 88–9; designers, 27, 31, 38, 69; documentation, 41; evaluation of, 42; existing, 27; fact-finding stage, 5; goals of (objectives), 3, 7, 23, 68; humanistic, 75–6; idealized, 68; needs, 4, 13; outcomes, 49; philosophical view of, 35, 42; planning of, 71; planners, 27; (and) syllabus, 3, 34–8, 41, 44; theoretical view of, 42
cyclical format see syllabus

decision-making, 175
deductive approach, 47
designers: definition of, 28; tasks, 32–3
dialogue (spoken), 30
directors, 80–1
discourse: spoken, 93–5; written, 93–5

191

Index

discrete points/units, 50, 51, 112–19

EFL (English as a Foreign Language), 23, 78–80
ESL (English as a Second Language), 23, 78–80
errors, 74–5
ethnomethodology, 118
experiential tasks, 96

face validity of course, 167
fact-finding stage, 5, 6, 29
foreign language setting 30, 38
formalists, 117

games, 82
goals *see* objectives, 24–5, 26, 30, 40–3, 51, 79; academic needs, 44; broad, 24, 25, 34; communicative, 49, 68–9, 79, 88; course, 26, 28, 41, 42; definition of, 40, 42; educational, 35, 77, 80; establishing, 24; in EFL setting, 24; in ESL setting, 25; formulation of, 41; general, 25, 30, 34, 40–3, 44, 89; humanistically-oriented, 77, 80; (and) objectives, 42; overall, 26, 30; personal, 51; problem solving, 51; realization of, 40; situational, 51; teaching/learning, 77, 79
grammar: discrete points, 50; pedagogical, 27; scientific, 27; semantico-grammatical, 90, 103; structural syllabus, 37; transformational-generative, 35; translation method, 35, 48
group dynamics, 96
group work, 31

holistic view, 73–4, 112–18; of sociocultural content, 135; of syllabus, 112–16
humanistic/effective philosophies, 48, 49, 75–6
hypothesis testing, 71

illocutionary force, 90
improvisation, 135
inductive approach, 47
information gap, 118
inventories, 19–21, 28, 107–12; notions and grammar, 108; socio-cultural functions, 109; themes and topics, 109

labor market, 12
language: analysis of, 36; context-embedded use, 72; context-reduced use, 72; form and function of, 115–16; national, 17–18; setting, 6–9, 31; societal factors of, 5–6; use, 32; (of) Wider Communication (LWC), 9–13, 14, 17–19
learners *see* audience: accommodating —'s interests, 153; assessment of needs, 123; autonomy, 102; role of, 42, 46, 48–9, 76–82
learning theory, 35, 64, 68, 71, 73–5
lexis, 42, 111–12
linear format *see* syllabus
linguistics: approaches, 46; descriptive, 64; rules, 48
linking elements, 149

materials: adaptation of, 30; audience for *see* audience; audio, 167; commercially sponsored, 33, 167; commissioned projects, 171; computer software, 167; development of, 18, 27, 71, 167–8; equipment, 32; evaluation of, 29, 31; gradation of, 64; hands-on, 167–8; method inherent in, 64; pedagogical implementation, 64; preparer's role, 147–51; presentation of, 164; reading, 147; selection of, 64, 150; specification in, 63; teacher-prepared, 167; team effort, 173–4; (in) use, 27, 29–30; variety of, 150; video, 167
matrix format *see* syllabus
mediation, 96
methods, 63–6